PRACTICE OF HONOR

DESTINY IMAGE BOOKS BY DANNY SILK

Loving Our Kids on Purpose

Culture of Honor

Practice of Honor

Putting Into Daily Life the Culture of Honor

DANNY SILK

DESTINY IMAGE® PUBLISHERS, INC.
P.O. Box 310, Shippensburg, PA 17257-0310
"Promoting Inspired Lives."

This book and all other Destiny Image, Revival Press, MercyPlace, Fresh Bread, Destiny Image Fiction, and Treasure House books are available at Christian bookstores and distributors worldwide.

For a U.S. bookstore nearest you, call 1-800-722-6774.
For more information on foreign distributors, call 717-532-3040.
Reach us on the Internet: www.destinyimage.com.

ISBN 13 TP: 978-0-7684-4135-2
ISBN 13 Ebook: 978-0-7684-8826-5

For Worldwide Distribution, Printed in the U.S.A.

1 2 3 4 5 6 7 8 / 16 15 14 13 12

DEDICATION

To Bethel Church: Thank you for your tireless efforts and participation in this grand experiment called "Bethel."

Acknowledgments

Bill Johnson and Kris Vallotton—Thank you for your courageous leadership!

Bethel's Senior Management Team—You are the "masters" at making all this work. It is a perpetual honor to work at your side.

Amy and Laurie—Thank you for your massive contributions to making this project come into being.

CONTENTS

PREFACE

*A*fter writing the *Culture of Honor*, people from all around the world are thanking me. Consistently, the feedback is about how much this book has radically reshaped people's view of who God is, how He loves us, and what to do differently to show the world a different Father. Another piece of consistent feedback is the request for a supportive workbook that will "Help us get this deeper."

I present this workbook as a tool to more deeply embrace the materials covered in my previous book, *Culture of Honor*. I hope and pray that you will assimilate the core values and processes into your life in such a way that it leads you to say, "I got it!"

Peace,
Danny Silk

Chapter 1

A SUPERNATURAL CULTURE

At Bethel Church in Redding, California, supernatural happenings, particularly miracles of healing, take place on a regular basis. These supernatural events are directly related to the *supernatural culture* the people at our church have developed for more than a decade. The heart of this culture is the conviction that Jesus modeled the Christian life for us. All the supernatural things that happened through Him flowed directly from His intimate connection with His Father, and that same connection was what He came to give us through His death and resurrection.

Sustaining a supernatural lifestyle where signs and wonders follow us, is totally dependent upon living out our true identities as sons and daughters of God. The leaders at Bethel understand that their primary role is to empower the saints to know God and to walk in the fullness of whom He says they are. As these core values have been taught and demonstrated, a group of people has grown up with faith and courage to bring Heaven to Earth.

REFLECT

How is understanding your identity in God connected to your intimacy with Him and your ability to live a supernatural lifestyle?

_____

_____

In order to help you understand Bethel's culture of supernatural empowerment, I am going to share something that happened in our School of Supernatural Ministry several years ago.

Every member of our staff shares a great delight in our First-Year graduates. We are so proud of their zeal and love for revival. After each summer break, our staff interviews the graduates returning for Second Year; this always reignites the staff's excitement to spend another year with the amazing people we call "our students." These Second-Year students are the cream of the crop and are leaders to our fresh batch of First-Year students.

One year we had two amazing First-Year students who were leaders in worship and other ministry activities. After graduating from First Year, they decided they would get married the following December, during the Second Year course of study. So they applied for Second Year and were accepted. Of course they were—they are amazing people!

Shortly after Second Year began, Banning Liebscher, the Second Year pastor, came to me and said, "We have a problem. I have two students who have confessed to me that they had sex over the summer."

I asked him what he was going to do.

He said, "Well, if having sex were the only thing going on, it wouldn't be such a problem. They stopped about a month before school started and are truly repentant. I believed him when he told me that."

"What else is going on?" I asked.

"I just found out that she is pregnant," Banning said.

Now this was a *situation*—an unmarried, pregnant, Second-Year Bethel School of Supernatural Ministry student roaming the halls. That was something we would have to explain.

I said, "Let's get together with them and talk about it."

REFLECT

If you were the leader, how would this dilemma make you feel, both toward yourself and toward the offending students?

What would you do in this situation? What would you expect from these students? What impact might this situation have on your actions or on school policy?

_____

_____

_____

_____

So Banning and his co-pastor, Jill Stocker, came into my office with the two students. I did not know them, and they did not know me. Neither of them made eye contact with me as they entered my office. It was clear that they were absolutely ashamed of what they had done, and had come in expecting us to punish them for their mistakes. Not only did they believe they deserved judgment for their sin, but they were aware of the common conviction that church leaders must protect the whole from the rebellious few. They knew they had been rebellious and that this would most likely be "the talk." What else could we do but tell them we loved them and show them the door?

I began by saying, "Thank you both very much. You don't know me, or what is going to happen here. Thank you for the vulnerability and trust that you have just offered. I know this is scary, and I don't want you to feel scared. We have not made any decisions, because we don't really know what the problem is."

I addressed the young man. "Now, let me ask you this: What is the problem?"

"Didn't Banning tell you what happened? Didn't he talk to you?" I could tell that my question made him uncomfortable.

"Yes, he has. Banning has talked to me," I replied.

He asked, "You want me to say it?"

"If you know what the problem is, I want you to tell me," I said. My hunch was that he probably didn't yet know what the problem was.

"We had sex this summer—a bunch of times!" he exclaimed.

"Now, I thought you stopped doing that."

He said, "Yes, we totally did. We stopped doing it about a month before school started."

"So, what's the problem?" I asked again, trying to send him searching further into his heart for the problem.

"Well, she is pregnant," he said, searching for the next thing I might not know.

I asked, "Well, is there anything we can do about that?"

"No!" he fired back, sending me a clear message that abortion was not an option. He was clearly frustrated by my questions. Apparently, he had not intended to do this much thinking through the process. He had anticipated punishment, and my approach was catching him completely off guard.

"OK, so what is the problem?" I asked once more.

He looked at me for a few moments, shook his head, and said, "I don't think I understand the question."

I chuckled. Banning and Jill chuckled. We all chuckled. No one seemed to know what the problem was, and everyone was wondering where I was going with my question.

REFLECT

Why wasn't the sinful act (sex outside of marriage) or the result (pregnancy) the problem?

_____

_____

_____

_____

Why was it important that the young man identify his problem, rather than just being told what it was and receiving punishment for it?

_____

_____

_____

_____

Finally I said, "If we were going to spend our time today solving a problem, what would that problem be?"

"I don't know."

I asked him if he had repented.

"Yeah. Of course I have," he replied, as if this were a "no-brainer" question.

"What have you repented of?" I asked.

After a long pause he admitted, "I don't know."

I said, "All right. Well, that is part of the problem, isn't it? How can you repent of a problem without knowing what that problem is?"

"I see what you are saying, yeah."

"So, we need to find a problem here to solve," I said. "That is what this is about. Let me ask you some more questions."

My whole plan was simply to ask him questions. I was not going to tell him what I thought or tell him what to think. I was not trying to convince him of my amazing perspectives or my powerful discernments. I was searching for the glory, wisdom, and capability in this young man. It needed to be raised to the surface so that he could remember who he was in this house. The shame of his mistake made him forget who he was. He thought he was one of those people who needed to be kicked and spit on, and he was ready for our leadership team to kick him to the curb like a piece of garbage. Questions led him, with the aid of the Holy Spirit, to search the wisdom and knowledge inside of him for a solution that would change his life forever.

REFLECT

Think of a situation in your life when someone sinned against you. Now apply the thoughts from the previous paragraph to that situation. Try to remember who that person "really is." What about that, if anything, makes you feel uncomfortable or violates your sense of justice?

_____

_____

_____

_____

Why are questions so important? Are you quick to ask questions or to offer opinions? Do you believe other people are able to solve their own problems?

_____

_____

_____

_____

When you are confronted with another person's sin, does it affect the way you see the person? What does this say about how you understand the origin of people's value and identity?

_____

_____

_____

_____

As the search for the problem continued, I lofted a couple of slow balls to the young man. "Tell me, did you not know that it was a bad idea to sleep with your girlfriend?"

"I totally knew that," he shot back.

"Well, then, what happened?"

"I don't know." He lowered his head, breaking eye contact.

I gave him a choice to consider and an opportunity to stay with me. "Is it that you don't know? Or do you not want to think about it anymore?"

"Well, it is probably because we were staying up until like 2 o'clock in the morning watching movies at her house."

"You think?" I raised my eyebrows.

"But I tried to leave. I tried to leave over and over again. I would say to her that we shouldn't be in this situation. We shouldn't be here doing this. I told her that we went too far last time and we shouldn't be doing this. But she would get so mad at me! She would call me names, tell me that I was rejecting her. And it was just hell for days afterward. So I just wouldn't say anything and stayed there instead. I am not saying that I didn't like it or wasn't part of it. I totally was. It just wasn't worth fighting with her about it."

"All right. So what you are telling me is that you were more concerned about her being angry at you than you were concerned about doing your job of protecting her from you."

Slowly, he answered, "Yeah."

"So what you are telling me is that when you are around angry people, it is easy for you to let them control who you are. Is that what you are telling me?"

"Yeah," he said sheepishly.

"So, all it takes for you to abandon your character and your integrity is for someone to get upset with you."

"Yeah." He was starting to get a revelation.

I asked, "Dude, is that a problem?"

"Yeah."

"So if we could build a solution to that problem, would that make our time today worth something to you?"

"Totally." He looked up again and made eye contact, trying to hide a smile. I could tell he was unsure about feeling better in the middle of a process that was supposed make him feel worse about what he'd done.

"Fabulous. Then let's work on that," I said, with a big smile on my face.

REFLECT

How was the problem finally identified? What techniques were used?

_____

_____

_____

_____

Why was the young man smiling by the end of this dialogue? What happened to his sense of self-worth and self-government? How did it happen?

_____

_____

_____

_____

I turned to the girl, who had been watching the whole process. I could see that she did not want to go through the same thing. I ventured in anyway.

"What is the problem?"

Quickly and defensively, she shot back, "I don't know."

"You don't know, or you are afraid to think about it?"

"I don't know."

I gently said, "I can see that you are scared. I don't want you to feel afraid. I do want to help you find out what is causing you to add so much pain to your life. Will you let me help?"

Eventually we got down to the revelation that she did not trust people. It was a stronghold in her life that showed up in numerous behaviors. She struggled with suspicion, and it kept her from letting people speak into her life. Several students had tried to address their situation over the summer, but she did not allow them to affect her decisions. She felt like these students were trying to control her; her fear blinded her to the care and concern they offered. This issue had wreaked havoc in her life for many years. She was fearful, isolated, often stubborn, and guarded. I got to the bottom of things with her through the same process: questions—lots and lots of questions and nothing more. They weren't any just questions; they were the right questions.

Asking the right questions in the right way is one of the keys to creating a safe place. A successful confrontation depends on how safe those being confronted feel. If we ignore their need for a safe place, we set them up to act like defensive, blaming, unloving, selfish people who are more interested in saving their own necks than cleaning up the messes they've made. We then completely miss who they really are and blame them for their behavior.

A process that respects the need for trust and honor will have an entirely different outcome because it allows people to be free—free from control, punishment, and fear. This is how we do Kingdom confrontation.

REFLECT

What is your gut response to the idea of giving freedom to transgressors? What about this, if anything, causes you to feel anxious or fearful?

_____

_____

_____

_____

Why is it important to establish trust and honor, even with those who have offended you? What benefit does this bring to them? What benefit does it bring to you?

_____

_____

_____

_____

We had two people in the same situation with two completely different problems. He was afraid of people being upset with him, and she was afraid of people controlling her. By the time we discovered these problems, they no longer expected to be beheaded over them. We had created a safe place for them to be themselves—the amazing people they truly are. It was then time to help them fix their problems and set them free from the shame of their mistake.

I asked them another question: "Who is affected by these problems in your lives? It's like you walked through a room with a big bucket of paint and then dropped it. Paint has splashed all over the place. Who has paint on them?"

They began to consider the people they loved who didn't yet know that she was pregnant. These were people who believed in them and had honored them. These were the relationships they wanted to protect—their parents, siblings, leaders in the School of Ministry, and leaders back home.

Banning, Jill, and I could see these two remembering all these people in succession. As each one came to mind, the students realized how much the situation was going to hurt others. They wept as they listed the names, finally experiencing the pain that the problem had created. Our team just sat silently, recognizing the godly sorrow that the Bible talks about (see 2 Cor. 7:10); it was leading the two students to repentance; we needed to let it do its work and bear its fruit.

They continued to sob. No amount of threat or punishment could have created what was happening inside them in that moment. It was a beautiful thing, and it all happened from the inside out. No one forced them to see anything. No one tried to talk them into repenting. All of this came to the surface because we trusted them to have a great deal of love and respect inside of them—and because we asked the right questions.

REFLECT

What happened on the inside of these two people to cause them to respond with the godly sorrow that leads to repentance?

_____

_____

_____

_____

How do people generally respond when they are told how bad their actions were and how much they have hurt others? Compare that result with what happened here.

_____

_____

_____

_____

_____

After they listed the people in their lives who would be most impacted by the news of her pregnancy, I mentioned some people who were important to me. "What about the rest of the Second-Year students? How are they going to be affected by this?"

"This news will totally affect them. They are our classmates," he said.

But she retorted, "Some of them will care, but most of them don't even need to know about it!"

"Ah, is this some more of that same problem?" I asked her.

"What?" she asked, seeming not to understand.

"Is this another instance of thinking you need to defend yourself from the people who most likely do care about you?"

"I don't know," she said, knowing she had been busted.

"You don't know, or you see what I am saying?"

"I see what you are saying," she admitted.

"Good. Thanks for taking a look at that. Now, what about the First-Year Students who see you as leaders in this community? How will they be affected by this problem?" I specifically addressed her with this question.

"What! They are a bunch of strangers to us! Why would they be affected by this?" she barked out, upset by my audacity.

But her boyfriend said, "You're right. We are supposed to be leaders in this school. They will totally be affected by us and what we've done."

I asked her what she thought of that perspective. She didn't like it, but did agree that it might affect some of them.

"Might, or will affect them?" I asked her. I was committed to pinning her down each time that issue of trust and vulnerability tried to keep her from showing her best self in the situation.

"Will!" she blurted out, followed by a half smile to thank me for not letting her get around it.

I then asked, "What are you going to do? You made a pretty good-sized mess here. We know who has paint on them. What are you going to do to clean it up?"

They went through the list and came up with solutions. "We are going to call these family members and we are going to write letters to these people. We will inform them of what's going on, repent, and ask them for forgiveness."

I asked them, "How much time do you need?"

After they conferred together, he said, "One week. We want a week to be able to contact our family and clean up this mess."

"All right," I said. "We will wait and take care of the School of Ministry students who are involved in the mess later."

REFLECT

Notice the many instances in which these two were given choices rather than answers (for example, "Might, or will affect them?"). What is the purpose and effect of giving choices like this?

_____

_____

_____

_____

In this situation, would you trust these two to clean up their own mess, or would you feel a need to make sure they did it properly? Why?

_____

_____

_____

_____

And so they did what they said they would do. Within the week, they contacted their family members and church leaders, and they also went to Pastors Bill Johnson and Kris Vallotton and some other school staff members. No longer were these people ready to be kicked out of the school. No longer were they people who deserved to be punished. They were met by a stream of loving responses and affirmation by almost every person. There were a couple of unfavorable reactions, but the couple had more than enough grace toward those folks.

You see, *shame is removed through love.* Shame tries to keep people trapped in their mistakes by convincing them that they are powerless and there is nothing they can do. When we lovingly removed the shame over these two people, they became powerful again, faced their consequences, and went around cleaning up their mess. In reality, cleaning up their mess was all they could do. They could not change the past; they could, however, go to those they loved and ask for forgiveness. In doing so, each was saying, "Please allow me to manifest my love toward you and protect this relationship. Please let me clean up the mess I made."

Love cast out their fear and made them powerful again.

POWERFUL PEOPLE:

Take responsibility for their decisions with truth and integrity, rather than blaming others or circumstances.

Refuse feelings of anxiety and hopelessness because they know they always have a choice, which gives them the power of self-control.

Do not need others to "make" them happy, but instead manage their own emotions.

Respond in relationships from the inside out.

Affect their environments rather than being affected by them.

Set boundaries with those who do not value what they're doing.

Are volunteers, not victims.

Direct their own lives and visions, knowing they can manage themselves.

Love and honor others, regardless of whether reciprocity is offered.[1]

REFLECT

Have you responded to people in a way that removes shame, or have you wanted people to feel badly for their sins? Do you believe shame and punishment are sometimes necessary in dealing with sin? Explain.

_____

_____

_____

_____

What does it mean for a person to be powerful? Are you a powerful person?

_____

_____

_____

_____

The following week, the two students returned to school. I knew how difficult this would be for some of their classmates. I gathered the class together and said, "Something is about to happen that some of you have never experienced before. It may be tempting to judge these two for what they are about to share. So please remember this: each and every one of you in this room, without exception, is a low-life dirtbag without Jesus in your life. Please keep that in mind while you listen to what they have to share with you. If any of you have judgments toward them, I want you to talk to me personally _before_ I hear it coming from somebody else you told."

Then I signaled for the couple to come up. The young man started by saying, "I want to apologize to this class because I know that we are part of you, and you are part of us. Over the summer we messed up, and now we're going to have a baby."

I was struck by his humility and vulnerability. He was truly repenting to this group of peers. He went on to say, "I've discovered a problem in my life that I didn't know I had. It has been causing a lot of problems for me. I am working on it now. I have more hope now than I have ever had about solving this problem. But as it stands, this is what's going on." He explained the whole thing. She stood there with him, humble and vulnerable, and after he had finished, she did the same thing.

I invited one of their fellow students, Brandon, who played a fatherly role in the class, to pray for them, forgive them, and restore them to a heavenly standard in relationship with the rest of the class. When he got up, 47 other students—the whole class—got up with him and surrounded these two, pressing in on them. Some wept. Brandon prayed prayers of forgiveness and love. He welcomed them back into fellowship with the community of the class. Someone else told them how much they loved them and thanked them for not leaving the school. Another student thanked them for trusting the class with this part of their lives. Then the students prophesied over them and the baby. They accepted the baby into the community. The whole class wept together. It was truly an amazing time.

REFLECT

How does the response of the students make you feel?

_____

_____

_____

_____

The room felt much lighter as people hugged and smiled through tear-covered faces. Then someone came in from First Year and said, "Hey! First Year has time to do this now."

"Do you want to do this now?" I asked the couple.

They said, "We might as well."

"All right, let's go."

I led the way. As the two of them headed toward the First Year class, the 47 Second-Year students followed them. The First-Year students could not help but be aware of the huge presence entering their classroom. The 47-student entourage lined the walls of the room like an army of guardian angels as the couple stood before 100 strangers and repented.

I asked Kevin Drury, a pastor who had taken a year off from his ministry to come to BSSM, to pray for them, bless them, and forgive them. As he got up, 100 First-Year students stood up and gathered around the couple to pray and bless them. Kevin prayed and prophesied over them, breaking the curse of shame and illegitimacy over the baby and severing the enemy's legal right to access and destroy the child through shame. It was a powerful time of love and reconciliation.

One hundred strangers embraced and loved on the couple that day. They had done all they could to clean up their mess. For the remainder of the year, they carried on as prime examples among our Second-Year students.

REFLECT

What do you think of the fact that this couple was allowed to continue as students? Does it seem like the problem was adequately resolved? Should the school have taken other actions? Why or why not?

_____

_____

_____

_____

Months later, the two were married. Shortly afterward, they welcomed a daughter into the world. From the day she was born, she had to fight for her life. The family lived at a specialty children's hospital in Northern California and sent us report after report saying that the baby was dying. Wherever we were when these reports came in—including in our church services and staff meetings—we prayed. But, for weeks, the baby continued to decline.

There was desperation in the voice of the new mother when we received the last phone call. "She is going to die. The doctors have all said that she won't make it through the night. Please pray!"

After this call, I specifically remembered and declared Kevin's prayer. I remembered that there was no shame on this child. I remembered that the enemy had no right to this baby. I reminded our team of the process of restoration they had gone through. Together, we remembered the honor and protection that we had given to this family. Our team prayed in our staff meeting and declared that Kevin's prayer canceled the shame. Death and destruction had no jurisdiction over the child's life.

The next day, we got a call. "The doctors don't know what happened, but they are calling our baby 'The Lazarus baby'!" said a very excited new mother. To this day, the couple's baby girl is alive and well. She is strong, beautiful, and full of life.

REFLECT

What does this healing tell you about the power of honor? What about the effect of shame?

_____

_____

_____

_____

The following year, this same young mother was one of the speakers at a Third Year gathering. She got up and, through tears, said, "I just want to thank the leaders in this house. You transfer strength and life from this culture to everybody who enters it. You build strength in other people. You've given us an inheritance. We will never be the same because of how you managed a situation in our life. Not many other leaders would have handled our situation the way you did. You will never know how deeply it has affected us. You gave us life in a situation that could have easily derailed us for many years to follow. You've given us a relationship that we would be willing to die for. Thank you!"

The stories of the people who comprise this miraculous Bethel culture illustrate the lifestyle and relationships that create an environment that draws Heaven to Earth. Without understanding the core values that drive us, you won't understand the fruit we are getting.

THOUGHTS ON BOUNDARIES

Like a city that is broken into and without walls is a man who has no control over his spirit (Proverbs 25:28 NASB).

Boundaries communicate value for what is inside of those boundaries. If you have several junk cars out in a field, it's called an *eyesore*. If you put a fence around those cars, then you have a *wrecking yard*. And, if you put a building around those cars, you have a *garage*. With each increase of limits, you increase the value of what is inside. When you raise the level of what you require before you will allow access, you increase the value of what you have. To all who are near, we send a clear message about the level of value we have for ourselves by the way we establish boundaries (emphasis added).[2]

At the heart of this culture is a regard for the value of freedom. We don't allow people to use freedom to create chaos. We have boundaries, but we use these boundaries to make room for a level of personal expression that brings to the surface what is really inside people. We understand that when people are given choices, the level of freedom they are prepared to handle is revealed. When people discover their true capacity for self-control and responsibility, they receive the revelation and opportunity they need to grow toward the freedom God desires for each of His children.

REFLECT

How were healthy boundaries maintained in this story?

_____

_____

_____

_____

_____

How do choices reveal the level of freedom people are ready for? How do choices help people become more self-controlled and responsible?

_____

_____

_____

_____

TOOL: QUESTIONING

1. Asking good questions begins with a purpose. When entering a confrontation, make sure you have a clear purpose in mind. In the case of the young students, the purpose was first to find out what the "problem" was.

2. Once the problem is identified, it is important to assess its impact. The next question should help identify those people who will now be involved in the "clean up," either because of their relationship with the person(s) at the center of the situation, or because of their intimate association with the problem, or both.

3. The next question invites personal responsibility and ownership for the "mess" by asking: "What are you going to do?" This offers the person a chance to realize that the solution resides within him- or herself and not somewhere outside. No one forces this decision; therefore, it is an act of great respect and care for those dealing with the problem.

4. Next, offer assistance and support by asking: "Is there anything I can do to help you in this process?" The question demonstrates that there is no punishment through judgment and abandonment but, rather, the opposite: an offer of partnership and care toward the powerful person who is attempting to bring reconciliation and restoration to affected relationships.

5. Finally, bring accountability with this question: "When will you have this completed—by Thursday or Friday?" Set firm limits if you have that role of authority. Otherwise, ask: "When is a good time to follow up on this discussion?"

TOOL: DELEGATING THE PROBLEM-SOLVING IN LOVE

1. **It all comes together here.** Confrontation is where all that you've been learning is tested. This is a good time to review the progress you've made thus far in this workbook.

2. **Who is doing most of the work?** In most confrontations, anxieties run high; therefore, love has to run higher. Too often, love and control become confused in our minds, and the confusion shows up in our behaviors during the confrontation. Remember that love creates freedom, but fear invites control. The key focus in helping to separate these two spirits is being ready to ask: "What are you going to do?" This question accomplishes two powerful and helpful goals:

   - It sends the message: "I believe in your abilities to handle your own life. I trust that you will figure this out and do what is best. I recognize that you want the right thing and will put to work all that God has given you to find and apply it."

   - It also sends this message: "This is not *my* problem; it's yours. I have no power to control you or your decisions. I love you and will help you, but I will not work harder on this problem than you do. If you don't see it as being important enough to solve, I will have to accept that and figure out what I will do next."

3. **Keep your love on.** Once the confrontation begins, it can be tempting to disconnect from people in order to protect yourself from their responses. It is also very tempting to let go of them when they disagree with your perspectives or ideas. And finally, if they make poor choices and there is no repentance, it *seems* smart to protect your heart from them, because they are obviously sending messages that the relationship is not important.

   - Always resist giving control of your love to someone else. Your love is the best thing you have, and it brings out the best they have. Stay in charge of your love, no matter what happens.

   - Bring hope to the interaction during a confrontation. You may be the only one in the room with hope. Often people who have made mistakes forget who they are and why they are valuable. Your hopeful expectations of a productive outcome will energize what would otherwise be a draining experience for everyone involved.

   - Stay tuned to the voice of the Holy Spirit. One significant advantage of asking good questions is the time it affords you to ask the Holy Spirit what to look for or what He is doing in the situation. Simply asking for His help in a confrontation is a key to staying in the Spirit of love and continuing to be a safe place for others.

DISCUSS

Discuss these questions with a friend or in a small group:

1. What about this story is most surprising? Have you seen similar situations handled differently? What were the results?

2. This story challenges common understandings of what words like *freedom, self-control, powerful,* and *honor* look like. Can you explain these concepts in your own words? Are there aspects that you are having trouble understanding or accepting?

3. What part of this story spoke to you most strongly? What aspects of it seem the most difficult? What can you take from it to apply to your own life?

APPLY

1. Think of a situation, past or present, in which someone did something that hurt you. Consider how you can apply the principles of this story to your own situation. Write out a "practice" scenario between you and another person in which you use only the principles of honor discussed in this chapter. If possible, share this practice with another person and get some feedback.

2. In order to change the way we treat others, we need to change ourselves. What in your life and heart needs to change for you to adopt the culture of honor into your everyday walk? Write down your thoughts. Then ask the Lord to give you a specific strategy for renewing these areas of your life according to His truth.

3. This week, try to apply the use of questions and choices modeled in this chapter in at least one situation in your life—perhaps with your spouse, your children, your parents, a co-worker. Share this with a friend or classmate and talk about ways in which you can improve your choice-giving and question-asking skills.

ENDNOTES

1. Danny and Sheri Silk, *Defining the Relationship: A Relationship Course for Those Considering Marriage,* 2nd ed. (Redding, CA: Loving On Purpose, 2011), 20-22.

2. Danny Silk, *Loving Our Kids on Purpose* (Shippensburg, PA: Destiny Image Publishers, 2008), 93.

Chapter 2

THE FUNNEL FROM HEAVEN

One of the primary factors that has kept Bethel Church in a state of preparation for and further stewardship of the outpouring of the Spirit is the "wineskin" of its leadership. Bethel's leadership has been established with an *apostolic and prophetic foundation* and with an expression of each of the other five-fold ministry graces described in Ephesians 4:11: the *pastor, teacher, and evangelist*. As a member of this team, I have seen firsthand how each of these diverse anointings addresses (through its specific area of focus and motivation) an essential part of the identity and purpose of the church. Without a complete, mature expression of the five graces that equip the saints, the people of God cannot be adequately prepared to receive what God is pouring out and release it to the world around them.

I am convinced that one of the reasons senior church leaders experience the disheartening cycle of great outpourings that gradually return to "business as usual" is this: the lack of understanding of the five-fold ministry, of leaders' own ministry anointings and callings, and of how their anointings shape the direction of their churches. Here I want to lay a foundation for understanding these roles and anointings so that leaders can recognize how they and others on their teams can draw on and administer the grace God has deposited in them.

REFLECT

What is your understanding of the five-fold ministry? How would you define the roles of these five anointings within the Church and within the local church?

In March 1995, I was working in a foster care agency in Mount Shasta, California. One weekend, we traveled to our hometown church, Mountain Chapel in Weaverville, California. After church, Kris Vallotton asked us to join him for lunch because he had a "proposition" for us. After some small talk, he told us that Bob Johnson (Bill's brother) was leaving Mountain Chapel to start a new work in Redding. He then asked if I would consider replacing Bob as the new associate pastor under Bill. My hands and nose got cold. Sheri and I told him that we would need some time. We could hardly believe what was happening, but within a few months we had moved our family to Weaverville.

One Saturday in September, Bill and Beni Johnson called us into Bill's office to talk. We figured there would be many of these "little chats" to help us get our bearings, as we had come into the ministry completely fresh and untrained. Bill and Beni seemed to be laughing nervously as we began the meeting. Beni told us how glad they were that we were there. She said that they had never felt the peace they now did and were so comforted by our presence on the team. She and Bill talked about our pastoral gifts and said that the people would be loved and well cared for under our leadership. I felt something rising up inside me as they went on, but it wasn't pride or great satisfaction. It was fear. The more they talked to us, the more I sensed what was coming. The bomb finally dropped when Beni said, "We've been feeling like the Lord is going to move us on from here. We've felt it for many years, but up till now never felt good about whom we would trust to lead the church. But now that you two are here, we feel so relieved."

I could feel the blood running out of my head. I felt like I was going to faint. Bill and Beni were laughing. I am sure my face was frozen with shock and terror, in spite of my greatest efforts to conceal what I was feeling. I asked, "Are you talking about five years from now? Three years?"

Beni answered, "February. We think we are leaving in February. We have no idea why, but that's the month we keep getting."

"February 2000?" I whispered.

"No," she laughed, "February, six months from now. 1996."

That was the last "little chat" about our coming on board. Sure enough, six months later they were gone. Bethel Church interviewed Bill in December 1995 and offered him a position as senior pastor. Just like that, we were sliding toward the leadership role as pastors. I guess we could have said, "No," but we knew the Lord had a plan.

After our meeting with Bill and Beni, I was angry, mainly because I was so scared. After I forgave Bill for luring me into a situation that I could not escape, I started to see what he saw in me: a pastoral anointing. He knew that our hearts would be focused on the people. We would make sure that their flock—the people in whom they had invested 17 years of their lives—got the best from us.

Thankfully, they were right. As the pastor, I began teaching and preaching material from my counseling background. I started building true identity as dearly loved children of God into the hearts and minds of the congregation (see Eph. 5:1). My schedule was filled with appointments to meet with people. This is the passion of the pastoral anointing: knowing that the people are healthy and strong because the Gospel comes alive as the saints manifest true love and freedom in their lives.

Bill and Beni had known that their church had been without a strong pastoral anointing for years. Increasingly, Bill's apostolic anointing had placed his focus more on Heaven's concerns than on human concerns. His associate pastor, Bob Johnson, carried a strong evangelistic anointing, and his focus was on the lost. The other leader was a prophet, Kris Vallotton. Because I wasn't replacing the apostle, but was providing a fresh perspective that met different needs, it was easy for the church to value and receive me as a leader. Bill told me that the transition of leadership was "scary smooth." Mountain Chapel was ready for what the pastoral anointing would bring.

We both expected fallout after his 17-year stint as the senior leader. There was none. This was my first lesson in understanding the nature and importance of each member of the five-fold ministry.

THE FIVE-FOLD ANOINTINGS

I can best introduce the attributes of the five-fold anointings by describing what might happen if they all arrived together at the scene of a car accident:

The pastor is the first one out of the car. He scrambles to assess the situation and begins a triage approach in applying first aid to injured victims. He gathers blankets, jackets, water, and anything else he can find to comfort them. He surveys the situation to see if anything is threatening the safety of those who are receiving care or those who have been drawn to the scene. He talks with the victims to find out their names, marital status, and whether or not they have children. He gathers vital signs information and any available emergency contact information in order to help the emergency response team once they arrive. He brings a sense of calm to the situation. As a result, each person experiences a genuine feeling of care and connection to the pastor. Meanwhile, he wonders whether he should have been a doctor.

The teacher is next on the scene. He studies the situation in order to figure out the cause of the accident. He steps back, analyzes the patterns of the skid marks and the distance each car moved after the impact, and estimates the speed at which each car was traveling when the collision occurred. Drawing from his deep knowledge of the driver's manual and traffic laws, he develops a theory about who was at fault. His conclusion is that, overall, drivers need more training and would most likely benefit from mandatory classes and continuing education requirements.

The evangelist arrives on the scene and asks everyone who is lying in a safe, comfortable place (thanks to the pastor) the following question: "If you were to die as a result of your injuries, do you know where you would go? Would it be Heaven or hell?" He then notices the large gathering of bystanders and people in their cars who have pulled over to watch. He begins to address the larger crowd with the same concerns, saying, "There are no guarantees that you will make it home safely. If you died on the way, do you know where you would go?" People give their hearts to the Lord right there on the side of the road. He explains to all the new believers that the greatest gift they can give is the gift of salvation. He trains them to lead others to Christ and prays for the baptism of the Holy Spirit to come upon them. Afterward he says, "That was great!" and decides to purchase a police scanner as soon as he gets back to town.

The prophet knew this was going to happen, because he'd dreamt about it the previous night. Because everyone in the dream survived the accident, he rebukes any spirit of death, and declares with great faith and unction that all shall live and none shall die. He also proclaims that there are angels surrounding the scene of the accident and prays that the eyes of all the people's hearts will be opened to see in the Spirit. Then he walks around and starts to call out the destinies of various people. He releases a spirit of revelation within the group. Finally, and quite naturally, he begins to ask around to find out who is in charge at the scene. When he discovers who it is, he discerns whether or not that person is God's chosen leader. Or, if he finds that no one is in charge, he appoints a leader.

The apostle prays for the injured. He invites the supernatural healing touch of God into the scene. He begins to testify of previous accident sites where he witnessed the manifest power of God. The faith level of the people begins to rise. He then asks if anyone can feel heat in his or her hands. He puts those who raise their hands to work praying for others to be healed. He demonstrates to all who are near that the Kingdom of Heaven is at hand. He then opens a school for those who arrive at car accident scenes and sends them all around the world to do signs and wonders.

This scenario displays the reality that each anointing is also a mindset. Each anointing determines how a person sees various circumstances and situations. As a result, different people will offer and apply different solutions to the same situation. No anointing is more important or more correct than the others. Each is simply one of God's gifts to humankind to help bring Heaven's perspective to Earth.

REFLECT

Using the accident scenario as your "guide," which five-fold ministry or ministries do you think your church's leaders fit into? If you are a church leader, which of these best describes you and those on your team?

_____

_____

_____

_____

In the past, have you believed that one or more of these anointings was more significant than the others? Why or why not? How has this analogy influenced your view?

_____

_____

_____

_____

APOSTLES AND PROPHETS

Before we explore the five primary anointings in more detail, let me point to the scriptural basis for the offices and the priority order of the apostle and prophet:

Now you are Christ's body, and individually members of it. And God has appointed in the church, first apostles, second prophets, third teachers, then miracles, then gifts of healings, helps, administrations, various kinds of tongues (1 Corinthians 12:27-28 NASB).

Paul clearly lays out an order of priority in this passage relating to the realms of the supernatural that correspond to each office. Hopefully, you could see in the previous illustration that the anointings on the apostle and prophet create a perspective primarily focused on two things: perceiving what is going on in Heaven and bringing whatever that is to Earth. The teacher is focused on being able to describe everything that happened accurately, while the evangelist and pastor are focused on the people.

Each of these areas of focus is vitally important, but in order for them to function together as God intended, they must relate to one another according to His order of priority: the areas of heavenly focus come first and serve to influence the areas of earthly focus. In First Corinthians 12:27-28, when Paul makes apostles first, prophets second, and teachers third, he is describing a flow. The flow streams from the apostle and prophet, through the teacher, is released in miracles and healing, and continues through helps and administrations, and tongues.

Tragically, in many churches today, the practices of teaching, helps, and administration have become largely devoid of the supernatural. It seems as though these gifts were plucked out of the list and separated from the *flow* of the supernatural supply of Heaven. In order to protect this flow, the Church needs to be founded upon leaders who carry a primary core value for the supernatural.

REFLECT

Explain the priority of the apostle and prophet. How do you feel about the stated importance of this order? Are there aspects of it that make you uncomfortable? Explain.

_____

_____

_____

_____

What are your views regarding the gifts of teaching, helps, and administration? Have you experienced these gifts in conjunction with the supernatural? What do they (or should they) look like?

_____

_____

_____

Rather than having the apostle and prophet at the foundation of Church culture, today's American Church has largely placed the *teacher, pastor,* or *evangelist* at the helm. But effectively divorcing the supernatural from ministry in this way has drastically impacted the general understanding of the true role of each anointing.

Today in most churches the role of a teacher is to state clearly and accurately the truths of the Bible in a theologically sound message that builds security in the lives of believers. The role of the pastor is to create a church that has solid family values and systems in place to nourish strong character and relationships. The role of the evangelist is to emphasize church growth and to train church members to share their faith and lead others to Christ.

The problem is that these are earthly focused models of leadership. Without the flow of grace from the apostles and prophets (who are not only focused on seeing what is going on in Heaven, but also on releasing that reality here on Earth) these models will inevitably lead us to focus on what we know God has done in the past and miss out on what He is doing now. They lead us to care more about knowledge than experience. It's even harder to avoid this imbalance when we live in a society that is permeated with it. Most of the schools, colleges, and universities of our land have embraced a dualistic worldview that separates knowledge from experience. This worldview reduces the goal of teaching to the mere transmission of information.

This paradigm is certainly present in the Church. The result is that much of the teaching ministry in the Church today is devoid of supernatural revelation and power. Instead, it is limited to what can be done from Earth's authority and production. But the five-fold anointing for teaching, one of the gifts of Christ (who modeled just what each anointing does), is very different. Jesus exercised His teaching gift by both *preaching* and *demonstrating* His message with miracles. Those who experienced His teaching were shocked by how different it was—different because He taught with authority (see Mark 1:22). He is our heavenly model and template for defining the ministry of teaching in His Church.

REFLECT

What is the danger in focusing primarily on what God has done in the past? In what areas of your life and/or church do you tend to be past-focused?

_____

_____

In what ways have you, as an individual and within your church, separated knowledge from experience? What result has that had upon your effectiveness in life and ministry?

_____

_____

_____

_____

The model of government in which there is a clear order of priority in the various roles is difficult to understand and embrace in American culture. Our American style of democratic government is designed to keep all of its governing members in a system of checks and balances, where each branch of government must be accountable to another branch so that no one governor, judge, or president can gain control of all the power.

I understand and value this ideal in an earthly model. Nonetheless, it is there in the Scripture: "_...first apostles, second prophets, third teachers..._" (1 Cor. 12:28). I believe that much of the Church has ignored this Scripture and has been using templates gleaned from Earth's governors in an attempt to replicate Heaven. But only Heaven's template can reproduce Heaven on the earth. When we use other models, the Church becomes nothing more than what people already expect from their earthly experiences. This is a huge and fundamental mistake with serious consequences. When we use human governing systems to define or reproduce Heaven, we're on the path toward implementing an inferior system. Heaven will not conform to or replicate an inferior system. Heaven must be the source.

We are not going to die and go to church someday!

In First Corinthians 12, Paul pointed to Heaven's template for government. This order is supported by Ephesians 2:17-22:

> _And He came and preached peace to you who were far away, and peace to those who were near; for through Him we both have our access in one Spirit to the Father. So then you are no longer strangers and aliens, but you are fellow citizens with the saints, and are of God's household,_ **_having been built on the foundation of the apostles and prophets_**_, Christ_

Jesus Himself being the corner stone, in whom the whole building, being fitted together, is growing into a holy temple in the Lord, in whom you also are being built together into a dwelling of God in the Spirit (NASB).

"God's household" literally rests on the foundation or leadership of the apostles and prophets. This design allows the Body of Christ to be built up into a *"holy temple"* and ultimately to become a *"dwelling place of God."* Isn't this what we all desire?

REFLECT

Have you generally thought of the Church as a democracy? Why or why not?

_____

_____

_____

_____

What reaction do you have toward this explanation of Heaven's government? How do you feel about the authority that this model gives to apostles and prophets? What about this, if anything, makes you uncomfortable?

_____

_____

_____

_____

According to Scripture, the foundations and leadership of most churches today (consisting of pastors, teachers, and administrators) are *disordered*. We've empowered the wrong portion of the list in First Corinthians 12 to be the primary leaders. The reasoning behind this decision is not spiritual, but earthly. James 3:13-18 warns us against this practice of pulling earthly wisdom into our lives:

*Who among you is wise and understanding? Let him show by his good behavior his deeds in the gentleness of wisdom. But if you have bitter jealousy and selfish ambition in your heart, do not be arrogant and so lie against the truth. **This wisdom is not that which*** *comes down from above, but is earthly, natural, demonic. For where jealousy and selfish ambition exist, there is disorder and every evil thing.* But the wisdom from above is first pure, then peaceable, gentle, reasonable, full of mercy and good fruits, unwavering, without hypocrisy. And the seed whose fruit is righteousness is sown in peace by those who make peace (NASB).

When Heaven is the model for our culture, the primary result is *peace*. Peace is the goal of Heaven because peace is the primary quality of the government of God. But disordered forms of government create *control*, which is their intended goal. Earth's leadership structure is motivated by the desire to protect the rule of those in office. When we primarily structure the environment of God's house to protect them or the will of the people, we've stepped off the path of the *"wisdom from above."*

When Peter tried to talk Jesus out of dying on the cross, he was trying to protect what he recognized as a good thing. His primary motivation was to keep the current benefit flowing to Earth. Jesus turned to Peter and said, *"Get behind Me, satan!...you do not have in mind the things of God, but the **things of men"** (Matt. 16:23 NIV). It is a clear word to all of us: Heaven is the model—not Earth.

REFLECT

In what way is the usual authority structure in the Church disordered? What effect has this had on your life as a church leader or member?

_____

_____

_____

_____

What is the difference between peace and control? Which have you placed as a higher priority in your personal life? Which is a higher priority in your church?

_____

_____

_____

_____

"FIRST, APOSTLES"

When I use the term *apostolic ministry* I am referring to the primary goals and objectives of the apostle's leadership and, therefore, *the goals with which all the people under the apostle align themselves.*

When Jesus taught the disciples to pray, He told them to pray: *"Your kingdom come. Your will be done on earth as it is in heaven"* (Matt. 6:10). His instructions taught them to long for Heaven on Earth. This core value is the primary objective of the apostle's ministry. Apostolic leaders are focused on Heaven, and their mission is to see Heaven's supernatural reality established on Earth. Having this motivation at the foundation of a church leads to an entirely different emphasis in the church's governing priorities. The apostle will make the presence of God, the worship of God, and the agenda of Heaven the top priorities in the environment. An apostolic government is designed to protect these priorities.

The apostle Paul refers to himself as a *"master builder"* in First Corinthians 3:10. The word used in the Greek is the word *architekton,*[1] the word from which we derive the English word *architect.* It is as though God Himself has given blueprints to certain individuals to reproduce Heaven on the earth. Along with the blueprints, the anointing carried by apostles contains a quality that stimulates and draws to the surface the diverse anointings of the people surrounding them. As those around a particular apostle begin to manifest their own unique anointings, it creates an environment of "subcontractors" who help the "master builder" to realize the blueprints of Heaven.

SEVEN KEY CHARACTERISTICS OF AN APOSTOLIC ENVIRONMENT AND CULTURE

1. It is heavenly rather than earthly. Worship and supernatural activity are priorities in the environment and the lifestyle of the saints because God's presence is the top priority.

2. It is effective. The saints are sent, as Jesus was, to destroy the works of the devil (including disease, sickness, and affliction); they live to demonstrate to everyone on Earth that God is always the Good Guy and the devil is always the bad guy.

3. It is joyful. The Kingdom of God is *"...joy in the Holy Spirit"* (Rom. 14:17); therefore, church is to be a place of exceeding, abundant joy.

4. It is love-centered. The primary emphasis of relationship with God is not service, but love. God's desire for this kind of relationship with those who don't yet know Him is made known.

5. It is empowering and seeks to build up and equip the Body of Christ to become a glorious and victorious Bride, regardless of the present condition of the earth.

6. It is influential. The Church is to create global awakening and impact.

7. It is legacy-minded. Descending generations must be equipped to carry Kingdom revelation.

REFLECT

There are many definitions of apostle floating around the Church. How do you feel about the definition/description presented here? What questions, if any, do you have about it?

_____

_____

_____

_____

Have you ever experienced being under the leadership of an apostle as described? What impact did that have upon your spiritual life and your spiritual gifts/callings?

_____

_____

_____

_____

The following reading, which is recited during offerings at Bethel Church, was written by Debbie Adams. I believe it best sums up the vision of apostolic ministry.

As we receive today's offering we are believing You for:

- Heaven open, Earth invaded
- Storehouses unlocked and miracles created
- Dreams and visions
- Angelic visitations

- Declaration, impartation, and divine manifestations
- Anointings, giftings, and calls
- Positions and promotions
- Provisions and resources
- To go to the nations
- Souls and more souls
- From every generation
- Saved and set free
- Carrying Kingdom revival

Thank You, Father, that as I join my value system to Yours, You will shower **favor,** *blessing,* and *increase* upon me so I have more than enough to co-labor with Heaven to see Jesus get His *full reward! Hallelujah!*

An apostolic environment is an exciting place because the focus on Heaven allows prayer, worship, miracles, signs, and wonders to become normal in our daily lives. However, there is one particular area the role of the apostle is not designed to address directly: the needs of people. When confronted with the needs of the people in Acts 6:4, the apostles said: *"But we will devote ourselves to prayer and to the ministry of the word"* (NASB). They were acting like apostles. The increasing needs of the people were a distraction to their role and anointing. It's not that they didn't care about the people. They did something to make sure that quality men in their community addressed these needs. But apostles must have the freedom to pursue Heaven if they are to effectively fulfill the apostolic call.

When an apostle pursues his or her calling without the other ministry graces in place, several real issues creep into the environment and threaten that leader's success: Unusual manifestations that are not found in the Bible, unprecedented scenarios and styles, an uncomfortable focus on the supernatural, and a noticeable inattention to the needs of the people begin to create friction. All the people can see is the growing distance between them and the apostle. As the people's needs go unmet, they begin to resent the way the apostle chooses to use his or her time. This may seem petty, but it is a real complaint that moves people away from an apostolic leader and a revival environment after a while. Open heavens and open back doors are the sweet and sour of the apostolic leader's experience. This is why apostles need the rest of the team.

REFLECT

Have you ever witnessed an isolated apostle (apart from the other five-fold ministry graces)? What was the fruit of that ministry in your life?

_____

_____

_____

_____

What do you think of the offering reading listed? Are these things priorities in your life and church? Why or why not?

_____

_____

_____

_____

"SECOND, PROPHETS"

The next vital piece in the government of a revival culture is the prophet. The foundation is incomplete without the presence of the prophetic anointing, a role that God emphasizes throughout the Scriptures:

> *...Listen to Me, O Judah and inhabitants of Jerusalem, put your trust in the Lord your God and you will be established. Put your trust in His prophets and succeed* (2 Chronicles 20:20 NASB).

Our prosperity comes through our agreements with Heaven's culture. The prophet's role is to clarify the reality of that culture and invite us to enter it. Therefore, success is built when we value the prophetic voices in our environment.

Our experience of prophetic leadership in Bethel's culture has come through many voices, including global and national prophetic voices, as well as equally important local and regional voices. Kris Vallotton is the primary sculptor of Bethel's prophetic environment. He is a gift of Christ to our house and to the Body of Christ. His role as a prophet in our environment has cultivated our expectation of discovering the heights and depths of the Good News. The Gospel is more than the words on the pages of Scripture. It is a reality that must unfold in the life of each believer. One of the primary ways it does so is through prophetic ministry that apprehends the promises of the Kingdom for individual destinies and calls them into reality through declaration.[2]

Kris's leadership and influence as a prophet have also cultivated our expectation for God to come. Apostles keep us believing, but prophets keep us expecting that God is coming. The dynamic ways in which God speaks to the prophet—including dreams, visions, and trances—create awareness of God's involvement with us. These supernatural tools introduce an infusion of sensitivity toward Heaven's activity and plans. But more than making us aware of Heaven through his or her experiences, the anointing on the prophet actually equips us to have our own heavenly experiences. Matthew 10:41 tells us: *"He who receives a prophet in the name of a prophet shall receive a prophet's reward...."* The reward is to see and hear what the Spirit is doing and saying. The prophetic anointing carries a *seer* dimension, and it gives people sight to see what was invisible prior to the prophet's influence.

Jesus, who modeled the office of the prophet, gave supernatural sight to others all day long. He often asked His disciples and those around Him: *"Do you not yet see or understand?"* (Mark 8:17 NASB). The answer was always, "No," because He was introducing an entirely different view of life. But that question led those same people to begin looking for something they had never considered seeing before. As a result, they received *eyes to see.*

The prophet and the apostle get along famously because both of them look into Heaven and then recreate, here on Earth, what they see there. They work together like a bow and arrow aimed at the same goals. Doubtless, this is why they are the foundation of the New Testament Church.

REFLECT

What influence has the prophetic had in your life and church? Has it been orderly or disorderly, when compared to Heaven's design?

_____

_____

_____

_____

Have you primarily seen the prophetic used in a healthy or an abusive way? How has this affected your view of this gift and role? What hesitations, if any, do you have about giving priority to prophets?

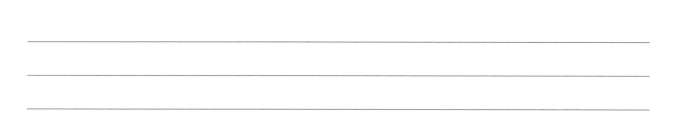

"THIRD, TEACHERS"

The teacher is generally accepted as the highest anointing level in the American Church. But it is only the third level of anointing—a C in a grade scale that keeps the Church only *average* in its effects and influence. Our need and opportunity to upgrade the anointing to an A is growing.

Our current Church culture places a high value on the sense of security we experience when we can prove the "right-ness" of that to which we have devoted our lives. In order to assert our faith, we assume that we must be able to argue our case to a logical conclusion. In reality, our need for so much certainty comes from the great *uncertainty* that arises when God's presence seems absent from our midst. When Heaven stops manifesting in the Church, Christians feel the need to *prove* somehow that they are reasonable in following Jesus.

When the power of the Gospel is replaced by our arguments, everyone should be concerned. When cancer, paralysis, tumors, and mental illness leave people's bodies and minds, no one requires an argument. A person experiencing the touch of Heaven is proof enough that Jesus is who He says He is.

When the Church insists on having a logical culture, we also demand a logical Gospel; therefore, we turn to the teachers. Most teachers are fixated on the written Word of God. They believe that the Word of God is the only source of life and truth on the Earth. Their value for the Word is much higher than their need for the supernatural. The teacher has a deep, driving need to be right and predominantly sees the world in terms of the "scriptural" and the "nonscriptural." Because the teacher is focused on the Word, the anointing of the teacher influences the Church to do the same. I am not trying to devalue Scripture, but I want us to understand how unimportant Heaven has become because of this dreadful error and disorder. The teachers, as the primary influencers in the Church, have turned our attention to the law.

When we focus solely on the Word, we tend to fight among ourselves over it. We then pull apart the Body of Christ because there is a right and a wrong. Each teacher is compelled to be right. As Paul said to the Corinthians, we have many teachers in the Body of Christ (see 1 Cor. 4:15). When the teachers disagree (and many do), there is division.

REFLECT

How much value do you place on security and logic in your personal life and church? How does this manifest, and what effect does it have on your spiritual life?

_____

_____

_____

_____

Have you or your church been quick to separate from others who disagree with you? What does this tell you about your leadership structure and values?

_____

_____

_____

_____

What then is the role of the teacher in the Church? In order for teachers to play their true role in Church culture, they will first have to be willing to pursue a supernatural lifestyle. They will have to become dissatisfied with the armor of their arguments and the lifelessness of their theology. They will need to risk failure and embrace mystery.

The anointing on teachers will always cause them to place a high value on education. They tend to believe that most problems are solved by training people according to Scripture. But the real change they want to see will come under the leadership of an apostolic and prophetic culture. In a supernatural culture, teachers will teach with supernatural results.

When Jesus taught a crowd about the Kingdom of Heaven, He always _showed_ them the Kingdom. His disciples were immersed in a never-ending classroom experience. Jesus took "show and tell" to a whole new level. Our teachers must put the "show" back into their lesson plans. As Bill Johnson says, "Jesus is perfect theology." If we see Jesus doing it, then we are on to something good. If we have not seen Jesus doing anything like what we are doing, we'd better ask, "What went wrong?"

Teachers must take the passion and the revelation of the apostles and prophets and show us how it becomes practical truth applicable to our lives. The role of the teacher is to help replicate the processes of the supernatural and then train and equip the saints to cooperate with those processes.

The love of Scripture and the knowledge that teachers carry help them to communicate complex processes in simple analogies and applications. Randy Clark of Global Awakening is both an apostle and teacher, and a prime example of this type of communication. He uses his understanding of Scripture to connect mysterious revelations to practical, daily life. His models for training people to pray for the sick are excellent and highly effective. He uses these methods when mobilizing prayer teams for ministry to large groups in his crusades.

A successful revival culture has teachers who perpetuate the supernatural. The days of teaching our limited experiences are over. We now must learn to teach how and what Heaven is doing every day to everyone.

REFLECT

Do you regularly act out the truths that you believe and teach? In what ways? Or do you feel more comfortable simply arguing theology with people? Why?

_____

_____

_____

_____

In what ways is the role of the teacher, when properly aligned, extremely significant? What result does this ministry bring in the lives of people?

_____

_____

_____

_____

WHERE DO PASTORS FIT IN?

Where will we put another role that has helped complete the disorder in Church government? The word *pastor* isn't even mentioned in Paul's list in First Corinthians 12, let alone numbered. How is it then that *Senior Pastor* has become the title of the most important person in the Church structure? I have a hunch.

When a group comes together, it isn't long before that group organizes itself in such a way as to get its needs met. Imagine a survival scene from a movie in which the ship sinks or the plane crashes and the people are lost. After any such incident, the steps are the same: the priorities are always food and water, shelter, safety, and then hope for rescue. The longer the rescue delays, the more another priority develops: the question of who is going to lead us. The nod usually goes to the one with the most aggressive plan to save the group. If that doesn't work, then the group begins to think about long-term survival. The leader they pick for the long haul is much more compassionate, steady, practical, and predictable. This leader will make sure that the needs of the people are met. He will ensure that they remain civilized and safe. He will be their *pastor*.

Pastors emerge as long-term leaders when all hope of rescue is gone. People gather around leaders they believe will tend to their particular needs. This tendency shows up in politics and businesses as well as in churches. If the people's primary focus is on themselves, they will elect a leader who has the same focus. It's as simple as that. If the pastors are not connected to the apostles and prophets, then their leadership will only lead people back to a self-focus, and the pastor will have to give them a natural alternative to a supernatural life. When a pastoral anointing is the primary leadership of a church, the people expect to be the center of the universe. And, unfortunately, the pastor thrives in that expectation, at least for a season.

REFLECT

How would you feel if the people's needs (including yours) were not the highest priority at your church? Would you be tempted to leave? Why or why not?

_____

_____

_____

_____

When the pastoral anointing is connected to the apostle and prophet, it provides another vital piece of the flow from Heaven to Earth. These caring, compassionate leaders are the necessary solution to the "back door" problem that apostles and prophets have in their leadership environments.

Pastors in a revival culture bring leadership to the people. These are the leaders who will be in their lives, homes, and families. These are the leaders who will sit with them and work out marriage problems. These are the leaders who will know about their struggles with employment or raising teenagers. If pastors can learn to maintain a dual focus on Heaven and on people, then they will be the ones who bring a revival culture to the everyday lives of the saints. Maintaining this balanced focus requires effort, because pastors naturally want the people to feel loved, discipled, connected, and protected. But when they are submitted to apostolic leadership, they are able to develop cell groups, for example, without making cell groups the primary focus of the church.

Pastors bring the nourishing presence of God into the lives of people. They connect the people to the supernatural environment created by the apostles and prophets. Instead of leading people to themselves and then showing them the love they have for people who are hurting, pastors begin to lead the people into the presence of God to find the solutions for life's problems. It is the pastor's good pleasure to see the saints find the green pastures of freedom and comfort that are made available by the apostolic ministry.

REFLECT

Why is the pastor more effective in helping people when he or she is aligned with the Heaven-focused environment of the apostle and prophet?

_____

_____

_____

_____

How does turning from self-focus to a Heaven-focus actually bring greater freedom and comfort?

_____

_____

_____

_____

WHAT ABOUT THE LOST?

Evangelists form the end of the funnel designed to ensure that Heaven's flow—from the apostles and through the prophets, teachers, and pastors—reaches its intended target: those held in darkness. The evangelist's anointing causes his or her primary concern and ministry motivation to be the souls of those who do not yet know Jesus. And realistically, unless the ministry of the Church is reaching those who don't yet know the Lord, the function of the other anointings is pretty pointless. I believe it is time for the ministry of the evangelist (which both reaches the unsaved and equips the saints to do the same) to be more deeply integrated into the larger purposes of apostolic ministry.

It is easy for us to believe that anyone can lead people to Christ. We have great faith that when we pray with someone to accept Jesus, the person is truly born again, right there on the spot. The culture of most churches has an evangelical practice among the people. Teachers teach it and pastors encourage it. The evangelists beat the drum everywhere they go: "We must go and win souls!"

But the bigger question is, "Then what?" The Kingdom of Heaven invading the Earth is the goal, not unsaved people invading the Church. The cooperation between all the ministry gifts is the only way to accomplish the primary objective of the Church. We must cooperate with the Holy Spirit in carefully and intentionally assembling the pipe that funnels Heaven and all its power and freedom to the earth. When we do this, the importance of the entire Christian Church being fully equipped by all the ministry graces (so that the Kingdom of Heaven "leaks" from our lives) will soon be a concept as widely accepted as praying a prayer of salvation.

REFLECT

What does the role of the evangelist look like in the apostolic government? What does it look like, practically speaking, for the Kingdom of Heaven to invade the earth?

_____

_____

_____

_____

In what ways has your church incorporated evangelism? How might the revelation of apostolic government influence your evangelistic efforts?

_____

_____

_____

_____

As I have been describing, there is a funnel within the five-fold ministry. When it is present and properly in order, it is as though God Himself pours Heaven into His Church like Moses poured oil over Aaron's head. God pours His supernatural world into His end of the funnel, and Heaven is processed and released to Earth through the five-fold ministry gifts.

The top of the funnel is naturally the apostles and prophets. Their attention is focused on Heaven, which creates a pull on the supernatural anointing of the Kingdom. The teachers take the revelation and teaching and bring stability and understanding to it through the scrutiny of Scripture. The pastors help people to partake of the banquet feast that becomes available to them in the atmosphere of Heaven on Earth. The evangelists "take it to the streets" and make certain that we do not forget the intended target of Heaven's glory.

The many wonderful effects of such a supernaturally charged environment create an overwhelming reality for people. "We are not in Kansas anymore, Toto," is the feeling many have when they experience a church where Heaven fills the room. It is the powerful experience of a wineskin that is fully capable of carrying and releasing the outpouring that God has promised to us all along—an outpouring that we were made for.

REFLECT

After reading about this funnel of Church government structure, how do you feel about it? What objections, if any, are you struggling with?

_____

_____

_____

_____

Would you want to be a member of a church like this? Why or why not?

_____

_____

_____

_____

TOOL: EMBRACING APOSTOLIC GOVERNMENT

1. Find an apostolic leader who releases faith for a supernatural lifestyle into your heart. Remember, it is not necessary for an apostle to be in the pulpit of your church. The apostle Paul influenced the entire New Testament Church from a prison cell for much of his ministry.

2. Absorb as much apostolic input as you can. Learn from an apostle how to see God, yourself, and the world around you differently from ever before. Allow this anointing to "tear the top off your box." Begin to believe God for more than you ever thought possible.

3. Seek to value and understand the role, impact, and impartation of each of the five-fold anointings. Refuse to choose a side or limit your honor toward the anointing that most reminds you of *you*. Determine that you will find a positive and life-giving place for each anointing to function in the environment around you.

4. Resist the temptation to turn your pastor/teacher into an apostle/prophet. Allow your current leader to function in his or her anointing. Honor your leader in that role. Your hunger for more will fuel your love and support for what your leader is currently bringing to the Body of Christ.

5. Pray for the outpouring of the manifest presence of God to come upon your church and city. Ask God to prepare the hearts of His people to receive and host His presence and priorities. Pray for the government of Heaven to be established on the earth as it is in Heaven.

DISCUSS

Discuss these questions with a friend or in a small group:

1. What is the difference between earthly governing systems and the Kingdom government outlined in the New Testament? Why is this important? What about this makes you feel anxious or out of control? What about it feels like a "breath of fresh air"?

2. What has your experience with leadership been—freeing or controlling? How does this influence your opinions about church government? Do you believe authority always corrupts people, or is it possible for godly leaders to maintain God's priorities even when they have great power?

3. How do you feel about the assertion that the Bible is not the highest priority in the Church? Do you agree that believers can be too focused on the Word? What do you believe is the proper balance? Discuss Bill Johnson's assertion that "Jesus is perfect theology." How does this influence the way you view the Bible and theology?

APPLY

1. Consider how the ideas presented in this chapter apply to your church. If you are a church leader, write out a plan for how you can begin to implement a shift toward an apostolic government. If you are not a leader, ask the Lord for wisdom on how to share what you have learned with your leaders in a respectful way. Consider giving your leaders a copy of this book to help them understand the concepts behind the practice of the culture of honor.

2. Make a list of ways in which you may have expected your church and your leaders to meet your needs. Ask the Lord to change your focus in these areas in order to see Heaven's priority. If needed, repent to your leaders for the unfair demands you have placed on them.

3. Begin to pray regularly (perhaps daily) through the offering reading from this chapter, asking God to renew your mind and heart toward Heaven's priorities. Ask Him for practical ways that you can make these Kingdom goals a priority in your day-to-day life. (For example, to engage the priority of miracles, you could begin praying for sick people to be healed.) Write down what He reveals and be faithful to act on it.

ENDNOTES

1. Biblesoft's New Exhaustive Strong's Numbers and Concordance with Expanded Greek-Hebrew Dictionary, CD-ROM, Biblesoft, Inc. and International Bible Translators, Inc. (1994, 2003, 2006) s.v. "architekton," (NT 753).

2. In his book *The Supernatural Ways of Royalty*, Kris Vallotton introduces the world to the core values and revelation by which he has established a prophetic culture at Bethel. (Shippensburg, PA: Destiny Image Publishers, 2009).

Chapter 3

GOVERNING FROM HEAVEN

*W*arning: I'm going to offend you for a few moments. I'm going to mess with your entire paradigm of justice. I'm going to take it out, laugh at it, tickle it—and then I'm going to kick it down the stairs. OK? You're going to have to chase it down those stairs if you want it back.

Imagine this. Your fifth-grader comes to you and says, "Here is my report card."

Immediately, you discover an F on it. *Aaugh!* The spirit of fear manifests in you, just as it would in the heart of every parent. *A fifth-grader with an F! He's doomed! It's over.* With fear gripping your heart, all you can think about is: *How do I control this child's educational outcome?*

That's what good parents think of: how they are going to control their children and steer them toward *their* (the parents') goals, because, after all, they love their kids. This is part of the lesson of love that most of us send to our children: *that which we love, we try to control.*

REFLECT

What would you feel and how would you respond as the parent in this situation?

_____

_____

_____

_____

_____

I'd like to introduce another option. Imagine the parent turning to the child and saying, "Oh, no! An F in fifth grade? We have an early bloomer! You're ahead of the curve—I knew this about you. I just want you to know that your mother and I have talked. We've figured out something here, and we want you to know this: we are going to love you no matter how many years it takes you to get through the fifth grade. And son, we figured this out too—if you wait just two more years, your little sister will be in your class with you. You and her buddies could go to birthday parties together and stuff."

Your fifth-grader is going to look you in the eye and say, "Years?"

"Uh-huh."

"It's not going to take me years to get through the fifth grade!"

Lo and behold, ownership of the problem has settled into the heart of the one who *should* own the problem.

REFLECT

How did the parent of the fifth-grader get the child to own his problem?

_____

_____

_____

_____

The way we parent our children when they make mistakes reflects most clearly what we believe about human failure, particularly sin. Many of us think that sin, mistakes, and falling short are more powerful than destiny. Many of us think that human failure is a nearly all-powerful force poised to overcome us; therefore, we believe we must manifest pseudo-power over it by getting into partnership with a spirit of fear! Yet when the disciples were going to call down fire on an audience that was disrespectful to Jesus, He just shook His head and said, *"You do not know what kind of spirit you are of..."* (Luke 9:55 NASB). Second Timothy 1:7 tells us we have not been given that spirit of fear, but of power, love, and a sound mind (or self-control). That is the Spirit of which we are.

When we are afraid of other people's sin, the fear makes us crazy, and we are not ourselves when dealing with their mistakes. As a result, we end up giving parenting and leadership in general a bad name. Do you know how many people are in counseling because of rotten leadership?

It is an all-too-familiar experience for us as leaders to cooperate with a demonic plan motivated by the spirit of fear when we are confronted with people's mistakes. Then we project onto God the idea that He's just as afraid of sin as we are. But what exactly is God afraid of, anyway? Nothing. He isn't afraid of anything because love casts out fear, and He is love (see 1 John 4:18,8). When you're feeling fear, that's not Him. If you aren't feeling the love when He's there, something's wrong, because that's Him—*love!*

So we have to decide: what partnerships are we going to make when we are in the presence of sin? This was the thing that made Jesus look like a genius. Jesus could come in and out of sinners' lives, and those people loved Him! They'd scratch their heads and say, "I don't know who that guy is, but I love Him!"

The Pharisees were more like, "Here, leper. Ring this bell whenever you come around, because you scare me, OK? Uh-oh, a woman on her period. Uh-oh, dead people. Where can we hide? Let's go into the temple."

Jesus had the love thing down, but the Pharisees didn't have a clue. So, in the presence of sin, the Pharisees were afraid. But when Jesus was in the presence of sin, He was the solution; He was the remedy; and He was *powerful.*

REFLECT

How do you feel when confronted with other people's sins? Do you feel an impulse to control them or the situation in order to ensure that the offense won't recur in the future? Why or why not?

_____

_____

_____

How did Jesus' lack of fear in the presence of sin enable Him to become the solution?

_____

WE ARE UNPUNISHABLE

Through the cross, Jesus introduced into the world something we still don't understand. He has made each and every one who has accepted His sacrifice *unpunishable*. It's not wishful thinking; sin does not need to be punished or controlled. It's not a powerful force over believers.

The problem is that we just don't believe this truth. Preaching this stuff is easy. It's another deal living it! Here's what the apostle John said about how we deal with sin after the cross:

> *My little children, I am writing these things to you so that you may not sin. And if anyone sins, we have an Advocate with the Father, Jesus Christ the righteous..."* (1 John 2:1 NASB).

John mentioned something we don't talk about enough. He said that Jesus is right there with us at every moment to help enforce the victory He's won over sin in our lives. After making this point, John went on to spend the rest of the book explaining that, because of the cross, our lives are no longer about trying not to sin, but about fulfilling the commandment to love. We are successful in fulfilling this command to the degree that we really understand and believe what Jesus' victory actually means: *"...He Himself is the propitiation for our sins; and not for ours only, but also for those of the whole world"* (1 John 2:2 NASB).

Propitiation is the word for "atonement."[1] It literally means that Jesus' death on the cross satisfied the need for God to punish sin in people. When Jesus went to the cross and gave His life as the perfect sacrifice, He ended an insatiable condition. He also introduced an entirely different reality based on an entirely different relationship between God and humankind. *He removed the need for punishment.* Therefore, He removed fear from our relationship with Him.

REFLECT

How do you feel about the idea that we are unpunishable? What about it, if anything, causes you to feel anxious or uncomfortable?

_____

_____

Have you lived as though you really believe that Jesus paid the debt for your sin and that you no longer need to be punished? Explain. How might this revelation change your view of God and your experience of Christianity?

_____

_____

_____

_____

First John 4:18 says: *"There is no fear in love. But perfect love drives out fear, because fear has to do with punishment. The one who fears is not made perfect in love"* (NIV). If we're going to lead our communities in revival and build a house for the presence of love, we have to know how to interact with one another in a way that eliminates the punishment option and the need to control those who fail. When we stand in the presence of sin and respond in fear and control, it makes us look like idiots. Those who sin do not need to be punished. We have to figure out a response to the real lives of the people around us, the real lives of the people we shepherd, the real lives of the people in the communities where we live. We need a response to sin that contains no punishment.

REFLECT

What do you feel when you read, "Those who sin do not need to be punished"?

_____

_____

_____

What sort of alternative response could we have toward sin (besides punishment)? Have you ever seen a different response modeled? What were the results?

_____

_____

THE FORK IN THE ROAD

The primary thing that will help us to change our response to sin is to gain a deeper understanding of the New Covenant that Christ established for us. The apostle Paul was passionate about revealing the choice between two different kinds of relationships with God. When we don't understand the nature of those two choices, it causes problems. Paul addressed the issue in Galatians 3 when he asked the Galatians, "Who has bewitched you? Who has allowed you to completely alter your belief system?" Then he diagnosed the problem: "You're trying to practice two covenants. You're trying to live in two camps." (See Galatians 3:1-3.)

In Galatians 4, Paul distinguished the Old and New Covenants by comparing them with the two offspring of Abraham. Ishmael, son of Hagar, the slave woman, represents the Old Covenant, and Isaac, son of Sarah, the free woman, represents the New Covenant. In verse 30 Paul quoted from Genesis: *"Cast out the bondwoman and her son, for the son of the bondwoman shall not be heir with the son of the freewoman."* In other words, the two covenants cannot coexist in the same place. You're either a slave under the law, or you're a free son. Light and dark have no fellowship. Love and fear have no fellowship. You can't do both; you have to choose one.

Paul concluded by identifying those who have embraced Christ: *"So then, brethren, we are not children of the bondwoman but of the free"* (Gal. 4:31). The next verse, Galatians 5:1, says: *"It was for freedom that Christ set us free; therefore keep standing firm and do not be subject again to a yoke of slavery"* (NASB). Again, Paul was saying, "You have two choices. You can live a life devoted to protecting your relationship with the rules. If that is what you choose, then you will find yourself back in the Old Covenant."

REFLECT

Explain the difference between the two covenants (two choices) in your own words. Which covenant have you primarily lived in? Explain.

_____

_____

_____

_____

The reason Paul was so concerned is this: the two different covenants produce different results. Earlier in his letter he mentioned having rebuked Peter, who should have known better, for trying to get Gentile believers to obey the rules of the Old Covenant. Paul then explained why this was causing problems:

*We who are Jews by nature, and not sinners of the Gentiles, knowing that a man is not justified by the works of the law but by faith in Jesus Christ, even we have believed in Christ Jesus, that we might be justified by faith in Christ and not by the works of the law; for by the works of the law no flesh shall be justified. But if, while we seek to be justified by Christ, we ourselves also are found sinners, is Christ therefore a minister of sin? Certainly not! **For if I build again those things which I destroyed, I make myself a transgressor.** For I through the law died to the law that I might live to God. I have been crucified with Christ; it is no longer I who live, but Christ lives in me; and the life which I now live in the flesh I live by faith in the Son of God, who loved me and gave Himself for me. I do not set aside the grace of God; for if righteousness comes through the law, then Christ died in vain (Galatians 2:15-21).*

When we start to obey the rules of the Old Covenant, we allow ourselves to be defined as those for whom that covenant was given, namely sinners. When we define ourselves as sinners, we, by definition, deserve to be judged and punished. When we protect our relationship with the rules, the result cannot be anything *but* punishment. Not only that, but when we choose the Old Covenant despite *knowing* that Christ has already dealt with the sin issue and opened the way for us to relate to the Father as His children, then we are actually saying that Christ's death was pointless. Without realizing it, we cut ourselves off from the only thing that can save us—grace.

REFLECT

How do you feel about this concept? Can you identify times in your life when you saw this play out?

_____

_____

_____

_____

Do you truly believe that grace is the only thing that can save you? Or do you feel compelled to obey in order to earn God's approval? Do you believe that your sin affects God's acceptance of you or the gifts He gives to you? Explain.

_____

_____

_____

_____

Unfortunately, the same issue still needs to be addressed in many of our churches. The downfall of the teacher's anointing is the elevation of the teaching of the rules to the supreme position in the church environment. This leads people to pay attention to and cultivate their relationship with the rules of God. We say, "Hey, it's not a religion, it's a relationship." We have bumper stickers, T-shirts, and car washes with banners proclaiming this truth. But look at how most church environments respond when someone breaks the rules. All the responses are geared to shepherding the person back into a right relationship—not with God, but with the rules. Punishment is the tool *par excellence* to restore a person to a right relationship with this culture.

The problem is that in Christ we have not been given a relationship with the rules, but a relationship with the Spirit. It is a heart-to-heart relationship that practices love. In Romans 7 and 8, Paul talks about two laws: the law of sin and the law of life in Christ. He declares that the law of the Spirit of life in Christ Jesus has set us free from the law of sin and death (see Rom. 8:2)—in other words, from the law of relationship with the rules. But that is not the relationship or the reality for most people. Most people have a solid relationship with the rules; thus their behavior is motivated by fear of punishment rather than by love.

REFLECT

What does it look like to live in a heart-to-heart relationship with the Spirit rather than the rules?

_____

_____

_____

_____

How do you think God feels and responds when you sin?

_____

_____

_____

_____

_____

_____

Paul explains that God's law is good in that it both revealed the power of sin in his life *and* his need for redemption. That was the purpose of the Old Covenant. However, the law itself could not bring about that salvation. Only in Christ's death can we die to sin and be free to live according to a different law. Paul says:

> *For I joyfully concur with the law of God in the inner man, but I see a different law in the members of my body, waging war against the law of my mind and making me a prisoner of the law of sin which is in my members....Who will set me free from the body of this death?* (Romans 7:22-24 NASB)

He goes on to say, *"Thanks be God through Jesus Christ our Lord! So then, on the one hand I myself with my mind am serving the law of God, but on the other, with my flesh the law of sin"* (Rom. 7:25 NASB). That which died with Christ is "the law of sin." In the previous chapter of Romans, he gives us a key for walking in the reality that brings us out of the Old Covenant and into the New: *"...reckon yourselves to be dead indeed to sin, but alive to God in Christ Jesus our Lord"* (Rom. 6:11). The word reckon essentially means to consider the evidence and make a judgment. God's verdict over every believer is that we're dead to sin in Christ.

Paul explains that the law was only for sinners. Since we're dead to sin in Christ, we have been delivered from a life of protecting a connection with the rules. Romans 8:1 tell us, *"There is therefore now no condemnation for those who are in Christ Jesus...."* Then it tells us that being in Christ Jesus means we are *"those who walk according to the Spirit and not according to the flesh."* Our experience of life without condemnation happens according to how we *walk*. We experience no condemnation when we walk, not according to a relationship with the rules, but according to a relationship of love. Being unpunishable, is the result of walking through faith and grace, in a relationship with the Spirit. It is all about my heart-to-heart connection...my union...my attention to a relationship with Christ.

REFLECT

How can you reckon yourself dead to sin and alive in Christ? What does this look like, practically speaking?

_____

_____

_____

_____

As we walk in the Spirit, the question we must constantly ask is: *How is my life affecting our relationship?* Keeping the law of life in Christ means that I manage myself in order to preserve and protect my connection to His heart. It's not about living to protect myself from the punisher when I break the rules. Many of us mistakenly believe that when Jesus said, *"If you love Me, you will obey what I command"* (John 14:15 NIV) it really meant, "If you love Me, you will let Me control you." If I still have a mindset informed by the law of sin and death, I will hear Jesus saying, "Keep your relationship with My rules!" (One sign that we're hearing John 14:15 this way is that we look for books about the commandments of Christ.)

But when we hear this command from the mindset of the law of Christ, we hear: "If you love Me, it will show up in your response to the things that I say are important to Me. The way you manage yourself in our relationship is going to be a clear indicator of your love. I don't want control over you, and I don't have control over you. This is why I've given you a spirit of self-control. Your attention to our relationship and your ability to manage yourself in this relationship will create and sustain the intimacy that manifests the law of life in Christ. Intimacy—'in-to-Me-you-see'—is how you learn what is important to Me; and if you love Me, you'll adjust your behavior to protect My heart."

REFLECT

How have you usually interpreted *"If you love Me, you will obey what I command"* (John 14:15 NIV)? What does this say about your relationship with the rules?

_____

_____

_____

In what ways do you live with the goal of protecting God's heart and your connection with Him? In what ways do you not live with this goal?

_____

_____

_____

_____

In the Sermon on the Mount (see Matt. 5–7), Jesus laid out some statements that look like a stricter version of the old rules. In fact, the kind of behavior He described would be impossible for any sinner to exhibit. But Jesus wasn't giving these commands to sinners—He was giving them to the sons and daughters of the New Covenant who would have access to an entirely new nature and supernatural grace. He was simply describing how these new people would behave. Remember, the Old Covenant was an external covenant, a system of controls designed to keep sinners in line. But the New Covenant is an internal covenant for sons and daughters who, because of their new nature, can be trusted with the responsibility of governing themselves. They are people who have access to the power of self-control *through* the Holy Spirit. The behavior Jesus described is evidence of the superior power to walk in righteousness—the power possessed only by sons and daughters of the New Covenant.

Obviously, we do face challenges in learning to walk in the Spirit; but they are not the same ones we face when trying to keep the rules. They are the challenges of dying to ourselves and exercising self-control. This is how we stay connected to the flow of God's grace that enables us to live sin-free lives. In a way, this law of Christ is harder than simply going with the "flow of traffic." But the rewards are infinite because this is how His Kingdom comes in and through our lives. The law that rules in the Kingdom is the law of Christ, the law of love—not the law of rule-keeping. When we align our lives with love, the Kingdom of love is manifested in us. This is why He said: "If you don't have love, if you don't have this, you have nothing" (see 1 Cor. 13:2-3).

You can be amazingly obedient to the rules and still not manifest the life of the Kingdom. There is no life in the rules. If you think you have a relationship with Jesus and love isn't showing up in your relationships with people, then I don't know what you have. If you cannot cultivate heart-to-heart relationships and practice intimacy with people, guess who is fooling whom?

When you don't know His love and how His love works, you don't know who God is. If you don't know God, He'll end up (at least in your perspective) looking a lot like you. You'll make Him up, and you'll feel like a rock star in the relationship. When we don't know who God is, we get scared, and we shape Him and our relationship with Him into "something" we already know.

REFLECT

In what ways is the law of love more difficult than the law of rules? How does this make you feel—hopeful or discouraged? Why?

_____

_____

_____

_____

Based on the qualifications described in the previous section, when you honestly look at your relationships with other people, what do you learn about your relationship with God?

_____

_____

_____

_____

We can only teach our kids what we already know. If we live in relationship with keeping the rules, we will not teach our children about relationship based on heart-to-heart connection; nor will we teach them how to manage their half of "us." The truth is that we give everyone in our circle of influence what we know, and this contributes to the development of a relational culture that is either rule-driven or love-driven. We talk a lot about culture around Bethel because it is so important to us. It is so important that we create and pass on life, love, and freedom—in other words, the Kingdom. If we don't understand why we're not producing those things in our environment, then all we will pass on is what we already know and have.

Generation after generation after generation after generation in the Church has lived life attempting to protect a relationship to the rulebook. You can say you're not doing that; you can say it all day long. But what happens when somebody breaks the rules? That is your barometer. What happens when somebody violates what you're living to protect? That's where it's going to show up. When the sin of other people scares you, it is evidence of how important the rules are to you.

The rules are pretty important in much of Church culture. It is time for us to admit that our fearful responses directly contradict the message of Christ that we are preaching. Scripture is clear that we have two options: we can choose to protect the rules and create a religious culture, or we can protect our relationships and create a culture of love. Only one of these options is the covenant that Christ died to make with us.

We can choose to protect the rules and create a religious culture, or we can protect our relationships and create a culture of love.

REFLECT

How do you generally respond when someone violates something you're living to protect?

_____

_____

_____

_____

In what ways have you passed along your relationship with the rules to your children or other people in your life? What effect has this had on the intimacy of these relationships?

_____

_____

_____

_____

TOOL: CULTIVATING INTIMACY

1. Choose to be honest. As difficult as it is, the choice is yours. Honesty isn't what you think of other people's behavior or the impact of their choices. It is the experience you are having with them on a *feeling* and *need* level. Stop judging other people when you get scared or hurt; instead, just tell them that you are scared or hurt. It's that simple and that hard.

2. Learn how to clearly and responsibly communicate what is going on inside you. Use "I" statements to open up to others when you are offended by their decisions. Try to use something like the following:

   I feel _____ when you _____.

   And I need to feel _____ in my relationship with you/in this situation.

3. Exchange truth. In order to create trust between people, we have to be able to tell the truth. When people get offended, they withhold the truth as a way to feel less vulnerable and more in control. The consequence is a breakdown in trust and the inability to reestablish it.

4. Allow people to clean up their messes. Everyone needs hope, especially in the face of failure. Be ready to allow people to recover from their mistakes and provide a place in your heart for reconciliation with them.

5. Ask questions that point to your heart. When people are cleaning up their messes, don't do it for them. Allow them to think through what has happened to you as a result of their choices. Do this by asking questions that show the hurt spot in your heart. For example, you might ask, "So, how do you think I'm feeling after that decision—happy or hurt?" or "How valuable do you think I feel now after we just went through that together?" Your questions can both reveal what is going on inside of you and create a place for the person to accurately respond to the relationship.

6. Learn to set boundaries. This is a much-needed, yet underutilized skill in cultivating intimacy and trust between people. Setting boundaries allows you to stay in charge of *you* no matter what other people do with what you've shared. By understanding that there is a line marking where your life "stops" and their lives "start," you will see the difference between what you can/should control and what you have no control over. This will help you to see the importance of providing others with good information about what you need to feel from them. In addition, it will give you the power to welcome reconciliation, or to protect yourself if they demonstrate that the relationship isn't important to them.

Discuss

Discuss these questions with a friend or in a small group:

1. Explain in your own words why fear and love cannot coexist. In what ways, if any, have you tried to make them coexist (or fooled yourself into believing they coexisted)? What insight have you gained from this revelation?

2. Removing the rules from the discussion, what does it mean to have an intimate relationship with God and to protect His heart? In what ways have you succeeded or not succeeded at this?

3. What sort of culture or environment have you created around yourself—one based in fear or love? What does this look like? What can you do to align your relationships with the law of love?

APPLY

1. Once you assess the culture you have created in your relationships, take note of the following: If there are areas and relationships that have been primarily governed by fear, make a list of these. Ask God to show you what steps you can take toward introducing a culture of love and honor. If appropriate, ask forgiveness from these individuals for relating to them out of fear and control.

2. Unlearning your fear of other people's mistakes will take practice, both in your mind and in real-life situations. Imagine at least three scenarios like the one at the beginning of this chapter, situations in which you are confronted with someone else's mistakes. Then come up with creative responses that are based in love. Begin practicing this in actual situations, too, with your spouse or kids or friends. When you handle a situation wrongly, do not get discouraged or give up. You can do this!

3. Consider how your view of God and His character might be influencing your relationship with the rules. Ask the Holy Spirit to show you areas in which you need a greater revelation of *who* God is and how He feels toward you. Write down what He reveals about His character and nature; then meditate on Scripture about these truths, asking God to continue to reveal more of Himself to your heart.

ENDNOTE

1. Biblesoft's New Exhaustive Strong's Numbers and Concordance with Expanded Greek-Hebrew Dictionary, CD-ROM, Biblesoft, Inc. and International Bible Translators, Inc. (1994, 2003, 2006) s.v. "hilasmos," (NT 2434).

Chapter 4

Dearly Loved Children of Light

"*For you were once darkness, but now you are light in the Lord. Walk as children of light*" (Eph. 5:8). Paul makes an amazing declaration and presents a piercing revelation with this statement. Many Christians are stuck in the revelation presented in the first half of this verse. We believe that the "nature" of humanity is dark, and we've had the most difficult time making the New Testament transition from dark to light. Because we have lingered so long in the mentality that says, "*The heart is deceitful above all things, and desperately wicked; who can know it?*" (Jer. 17:9), we've failed to cultivate the truth that we are children of light. Yes, we once *were* darkness, but that nature has completely changed. Our fear of sin must be removed and our offenses disarmed before we will allow Heaven to govern through us on the earth.

When people break the rules, it is offensive to human nature. The world is offended by sin. Look at the headlines in your newspaper. People love this stuff. It is natural to be offended when someone breaks the rules. We put people in prison and call them *offenders*. Our society is filled with sinners practicing sin, and naturally, our society is caught in a relationship with the rules. Even lawlessness is a relationship with the rules. That's the only option our society has. And people love to play judge. That's what headlines and newscasts are for, to help us sharpen our judgment skills.

REFLECT

Do you feel a sense of justice or satisfaction when a wrong-doer is exposed? Why or why not?

_____

_____

_____

_____

Do you believe that human nature and the human heart are inherently dark? What effect does the cross of Christ have on that reality? What does it mean that your nature has been completely changed?

_____

_____

_____

_____

We as believers living in this wider culture have to be aware of our natural inclination to be offended. We must also be aware of the effects of offense upon us. Offense justifies the decision to withhold our love. When others break the rules, we feel "entitled" to withhold our love from them, because we see those who fail as being unworthy of love and deserving of punishment. In fact, what punishment most often looks like is the withholding of love. Unfortunately, when we withhold love, anxiety fills the void, and a spirit of fear directs our behavior toward our offenders.

When we are afraid, we want control. Our responses to the sins of other people form a set of controls that help us feel like we are still in charge. The typical practice of family, church, and government is to set a series of behaviors called punishments in front of offenders. Offenders are then required to walk through these behaviors in order to prove that the family, church, and government are still in charge in their respective environments. In this way, we help to confirm what offenders already believe: that they are powerless to change and powerless to take responsibility for their behavior. This whole business is just what Jesus died to get rid of. He's introduced a whole other world with a whole other way.

REFLECT

In what way does offense justify the decision to withhold love? When have you done this in your life? When has someone else done it to you? What were the relational consequences?

_____

_____

_____

_____

Why does punishment cause a person to feel powerless? What is the new way that Jesus introduced? What does it look like?

_____

_____

_____

_____

A MAN AFTER GOD'S OWN HEART

Though he lived under the Old Covenant, David was a man who valued his relationship with God more than he valued the rules. In Second Samuel 11, we read the story of the time when David should have gone to war, but instead stayed home and sent out Joab to do the work. With free time on his hands, David walked headlong into temptation: *"Then it happened one evening that David arose from his bed and walked on the roof of the king's house. And from the roof he saw a woman bathing, and the woman was very beautiful to behold"* (2 Sam. 11:2).

David asked around, saying, "Who's that?"

And they said, "Well, that's Uriah's wife."

Uriah the Hittite was one of David's mighty men—one of his friends. We read in verse 4: *"Then David sent messengers and took her; and she came to him, and he lay with her...."*

If we know anything about Bathsheba, we know that she was an amazing woman because of who she was married to. Uriah was stellar. He would never have married some loser. David took Bathsheba, brought her to his room, and lay with her. It is quite likely that David raped Bathsheba. Verse 4 goes on to say that *"...when she had purified herself from her uncleanness, she returned to her house"* (NASB), only to send David a message some time later that she was pregnant. This did not happen in the course of a weekend. It took months. This was before the days of blue-strip pregnancy tests; no plus and minus could be seen. I'm sure Bathsheba waited until she knew for certain before telling the king that she was pregnant, so it had to be months after their original encounter.

When David found out he said, "Where's Uriah? Hey, go get him and let's give him some time on leave."

When Uriah showed up, David as much as said, "You amazing man you! Come here. I just love you. Thanks for all that you're doing to support the war effort. Now, go sleep with your wife. I heard she's been eating a lot lately. I think she's kind of upset. You might want to comfort her. I need some help covering up the consequence of my sin."

But Uriah wouldn't do it. Instead, he slept on the front steps of the king's house and said, "Why should I go sleep with my wife in my bed when the men are lying in a field? I won't go" (see 2 Sam. 11:9-11).

David thought, *Dang! A man with character. I wasn't expecting that.* So he decided, "Hey, let's have a little party. Maybe if I can get him drunk, I can get him to leave his senses, and then I can get him to cover up my sin." That time Uriah did sleep in a bed—in the servant's quarters.

What was David going to do? "OK, we're running out of time. She's going to deliver soon if you don't get this together. Here, Uriah, take this note and give it to Joab. Take your death warrant and hand it to your commander." This did not happen in a weekend, and it wasn't just a little aberration in David's character. No. David was practicing something. Sure enough, Joab sent Uriah to the frontlines, pulled back the troops, and Uriah was killed. (See Second Samuel 11:12-17.)

REFLECT

How does this telling of David's story impact you? In what ways, if any, does it modify your opinion of him? Why or why not?

_____

_____

_____

_____

At this point, it was time for the situation to be confronted. Nathan the prophet went to the king, and David spent seven days repenting on the floor. Yet David's son, the baby born to

Bathsheba, still died as Nathan said he would. Then we read Second Samuel 12:24: *"Then David comforted Bathsheba his wife, and went in to her and lay with her. So she bore a son, and he called his name Solomon...."*

Yes, the child died. But something doesn't quite add up here. Where was the punishment in this story—punishment that really "fit the crime?" We usually don't feel the weight of what David did to Uriah and Bathsheba because of all the other great things he did and because God said David was a man after His heart (see 1 Sam. 13:14; Acts 13:22). But we need to see that if David were the president of the United States, he would be the old-time equivalent of Bill Clinton (excepting that, as far as we know, Bill Clinton has never killed one of his close friends and married his friend's wife).

Do you remember holding any offense against Bill Clinton? Do you remember rejoicing at any thoughts you may have had about his being punished?

REFLECT

What is the difference between David and Bill Clinton?

_____

_____

_____

_____

If David were a modern Church leader, what, in your opinion, would be the right way to handle the situation with Bathsheba? In what ways does your verdict differ from God's (as recorded in the Bible) and why?

_____

_____

_____

_____

There are other examples worth noting in Scripture, examples that defy the expectations of justice created by the rules. Take Abigail. Abigail was, basically, an un-submissive wife. She took her husband's stuff and gave it to David, who was very upset. He was coming to kill her husband, Nabal, because he refused to give David and his men some food. So Abigail made a last-minute, behind-her-husband's-back delivery. This made her a rebellious, un-submissive wife according to the rules. And what was the response? God killed her jerk husband, and she married David (see 1 Sam. 25).

Then there was Peter. In Matthew 26, Jesus told him, "Peter, you're going to deny Me."

Peter said, "No way!"[1]

Jesus had already said, in Matthew 10:33: "And if you deny Me before people, I will deny you before My Father." Sure enough, Peter denied Him. What did Jesus do?

"Peter, do you love Me? Peter, will you protect the things that I told you were so important to Me? Peter, will you manage your life in such a way that you will protect Me?"

Peter confessed his love, in essence, saying, "Yes, Lord. Yes, I will" (See John 21:15-17.)

The adulteress—what was Jesus' response to her? "*...Go and sin no more*" (John 8:11). Wow! That's going to leave a mark! Or no, actually it's not—certainly not the kind of mark the rest of the people were hoping to make on her.

REFLECT

What do the examples of Abigail, Peter, and the adulteress show you about God's sense of justice?

_____

_____

_____

_____

_____

What, if anything, about these examples offends you? In what ways do they seem unfair or cause you to feel anxious?

_____

_____

_____

_____

_____

WHAT'S THE DIFFERENCE?

Why does God respond differently to different people's mistakes? Why did David and Peter get a different deal from the one they deserved? Why did they get a different deal from other people who made the same mistakes, or even less serious mistakes? What was the difference between David and Saul, for example? David killed a man; Saul just failed to kill everybody he was supposed to kill. What was the difference between Peter and Judas? Peter denied Jesus three times; Judas only betrayed Jesus once.

The real difference is vitally important; it is not in their sin, but in what they did afterward. It is *repentance*. But know this: repentance only works when the priority of the environment is a heart-to-heart connection.

Repentance does not satisfy the broken rules. Repentance will not work in an environment where you are protecting a relationship with the rules. In a rule-driven environment, repentance has a different meaning. It signifies your willingness to be punished. You are repentant when you allow me to inflict my punishments upon you for whatever offense you have committed against me. The issue of the heart that led you to make the mistake in the first place is never dealt with, because the issues of relationship and love are never touched.

In a rule-driven culture, the general attitude toward a repentant person is: "You have surrendered your will to me in our environment. I'll never be able to trust you though, because you have proven yourself to be a lawbreaker, and that fact will rest in my memory for a really long time. Until I begin to forget about how scared I am of you, I'll never be able to empower you again."

This is the attitude that presides over what we typically call the "restoration process."

True repentance is a gift. It's not your option. It's not your call. It is a gift that comes in a relationship. There's no place for repentance in the rules; there's only room for punishment. If you break our rules, then you pay our price. You do the crime, so you do the time. That's just how it works. You pay the price in order to assuage the anxieties of the people in the environment who live within those rules.

When we practice this in the Church, we allow ourselves to be defined by the limits of earthly government. When you break the law, the best Earth's government can do is to say, "We hurt them sufficiently so that you all would calm down."

REFLECT

Why doesn't repentance satisfy the broken rules? What does satisfy the broken rules?

_____

_____

_____

What has your experience been with repentance? Has it seemed like a powerful tool? What difference has repentance made in your life? What does this tell you about your environment and your relationship with the rules?

_____

_____

_____

_____

The gift of repentance creates the opportunity for true restoration. In fact, it is absolutely necessary in order to heal a relationship that has been hurt by sinful behavior. True repentance can only come through a relationship with God in which we come into contact with the grace of God to change. David spent seven days on the ground repenting to God. Saul also tried to repent to Samuel for breaking the rules (see 1 Sam. 15). But when David got off the ground, he was another man. How do we know that? He never did it again. There was no other Bathsheba.

So what is true restoration? An old meaning of the word *restoration* refers to the process of finding someone with royal blood who had been ousted from rule, and restoring that person to the throne. When dealing with leaders in the Church who have broken the rules, our process of restoration rarely resembles the returning of monarchs to their places of authority. Most fallen leaders leave their churches or denominations and make "fresh starts" elsewhere. That means that they find a group of people who are not afraid of them breaking the rules again.

But when God restores those who have repented, His restoration process *does* look like the reestablishing of rulership in the life of a royal family member. The restored believer can say, "I am now a son of God again." Restoration for the believer is always a restoration of relationship. This is for two reasons: (1) restoration is defined by the cross and (2) restoration to relationship is what the cross did.

After John declared that Jesus became the propitiation for our sins, he concluded: *"If God so loved us"*—that is, if God was so willing to protect His relationship with us instead of protecting our relationship with His rules—*"we also ought to love one another"* (1 John 4:11). In other words, we ought to love one another in the same way. The standard of Heaven's government is to cultivate and protect our relationship with God, with love, and with each other. If we can't do it, we won't reflect Heaven to the society we live in. We will just have stricter rules that offend us more quickly and more often. And we will become wildly famous for being offended judges.

REFLECT

Explain true restoration in your own words. In what ways does this differ from your experience of the restoration process in the Church?

_____

_____

_____

_____

Are you known as someone who quickly becomes an offended judge? Why or why not?

_____

_____

_____

_____

Jesus provided a way for us to become free from the law that keeps us tied to an earthly model of government, particularly from how that model responds to sin. The reason an apostolic and prophetic environment is so important is that it constantly renews and refreshes our awareness of and trust in the core values of Heaven, so that we can bring them to Earth. It seems clear to me that the very best we can do in an environment where teachers and pastors lead is to justify the behavior of utilizing Earth's models to deal with God's people. When we implement the core values of Heaven into the culture of our congregations and families (including the core value that we are unpunishable), I believe these cultures will truly be reformed and people will experience life in a completely different way.

REFLECT

In what ways does an apostolic government change the way we view sin and repentance?

_____

_____

_____

How will the reality of being unpunishable enable people to experience life in a "completely different way"?

_____

_____

_____

_____

FULL OF LIGHT

I want to tell you a little story that encapsulates what heavenly restoration looks like. A friend of mine, a pastor and teacher (one of the most capable, brilliant teachers that I know), called me one day and said, "I have a worship leader who just confessed to his wife about an immoral relationship. It's been going on for four years with his wife's best friend. He and his wife were actually mentors to this woman and her husband when the couple came into the church and took a staff position working with our youth. We don't know what to do, because this isn't just your run-of-the-mill worship leader. This guy is amazing. He has been taking our church to new places in God. Over the past four years, the anointing on our house has increased. We've started a school of ministry, and he and his wife run it. This is our third year. We've almost doubled the enrollment of our school in three years. This couple is leading in creating an amazing environment."

This pastor had called me because he knew what had to happen when the truth came out; he knew what had to happen when you break the rules and you're in a relationship with the rules. They had to put this man through the "restoration process." But this pastor also knew that the restoration process we had at Bethel looked different from the one he had always known. So he asked if I would be willing to meet with this couple first and then give him some insight about how to proceed.

REFLECT

What would you advise this pastor to do? Why?

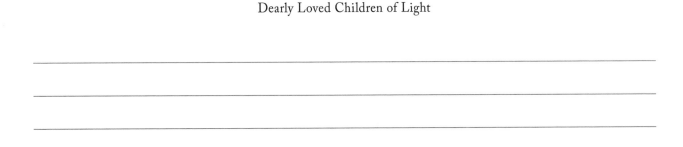

My wife, Sheri, and I met with the couple about two days later. When they walked in the door, the wife looked as though she'd been crying for a week. He was wracked with shame. He knew that he needed to be punished. She was just distraught; her heart was broken. All the trust that she had ever held was crushed. *She* was going to lose *her* valuable ministry in the church. *Her* life had been ended because of *his* incredible selfishness.

We sat and listened to them for a few minutes. He did his best to let us know what an evil dirtbag he was. "I knew better. I knew what I was doing. I was hiding it. There's a war inside of me. I've had this problem my whole life. Eighteen years ago when we got married and she was pregnant with our first child, I committed adultery with her best friend then, too." He continued to attempt to convince us that he deserved to be punished.

Eventually Sheri prophesied over him: "I see this hand coming out of the sky, grabbing this handle, and flipping this switch, and then all the lights just coming on. It is like you are full of light and everything is completely different. That is what the Lord is going to do."

He said, "That's really sweet of you to say that. I just can't believe that right now. I feel a million miles from that place right now."

We were watching a clash of two kingdoms: love and fear, freedom and control, light and dark. The earthly kingdom that this couple knew was severely limited in trying to restore a child of light. Once again, the truth is that *"You **were** formerly darkness, but now you **are** Light in the Lord; walk as children of light"* (Eph. 5:8 NASB). But dearly loved children of light cannot be governed by the very best darkness we can find. The most merciful, fair, just, capitalistic, democratic darkness cannot govern children of light.

REFLECT

What does it mean that earthly kingdoms (darkness) cannot govern children of light? Why is this true? How should it influence your view of children of light?

_____

_____

Consider the difference between the man's depiction of himself as a dirtbag and the prophetic word that God released. What does this show you about the difference between the kingdoms of love and fear, and freedom and control?

_____

_____

_____

_____

Sheri and I had as our goal inviting them to experience the power of an apostolic environment that has made the resources of Heaven permanently within reach. We had access to the resource of light in an atmosphere that requires light. When Heaven invades Earth, it trumps the limitations of natural people and natural perspectives.

We did not believe that what this man had done was evidence of his true identity. Paul said we once _were_ darkness, and we now _are_ light (see Eph. 5:8). Having darkness in us doesn't change our true identity. Once, as I was walking, I stepped on a board, and a nail went through my foot. I could clearly see that a nail had entered my foot. Yet never once did I think, "I'm a nail!" I was, however, very interested in getting that nail out of my foot.

When a child of light discovers darkness in himself or herself, it forces the question: "What are _you_ going to do?" When we come alongside people in this kind of situation, we can help them hear God's question by sending this clear message: "It isn't my job to control you. I'm not scared. What are _you_ going to do?"

REFLECT

To what degree do you find your identity in your actions or achievements? How do you feel about yourself when you fail? How does the nail-in-the-foot illustration change your view of sin?

_____

_____

_____

When you sin, why does God ask, "What are you going to do?" How does this make you feel?

_____

_____

_____

_____

We began the restoration process with this couple by asking some questions. We brought our light with us. Living in an apostolic governing system helps us to pull light from Heaven into our pastoral relationships naturally. Therefore, we have a process that heals our relationships with people who break the rules. It makes us powerful in the presence of sin. We're not afraid of sin. Sin is nothing! Sin is darkness! One flick of the switch and—*click*—it's over!

So I asked the question that I ask everyone in these situations: "What is the problem? What is the problem that would drive a man to do such destructive stuff to his family, to his life, to the church he loves, and to his peace with God? What would make a man get there? What's the problem?"

"I don't know," he responded dejectedly.

"Have you repented?"

"Yes," he replied with adamant fervor, though his tone betrayed doubt that this repentance would stand up to a test.

"Of what?" I asked, boxing him in.

He looked at me, unsure whether I was for him or against him. He answered, "I don't know."

"That's what I was thinking. How is this going to change if you don't even know how to repent?" I asked.

"I don't know," he said, resigned.

"That's what I was thinking, too!"

Sheri and I looked at this man from a perspective of light. We intended to solve this issue from a heavenly context, because that was part of our culture. It was natural for us to approach sin and failure from a perspective that makes God more powerful than sin. The man, on the other hand, was convinced that he was darkness personified. He knew that the government of Earth was waiting to have its way with him. He agreed with the paradigm of Earth and was ready to welcome its verdict of judgment. It was our job to move him to see himself from another vantage point. He needed to believe he was a dearly loved child of light.

REFLECT

Do you truly believe that God is more powerful than sin? How does this manifest in your daily life?

_____

_____

_____

_____

_____

I continued questioning the man. "One more time: what do you think the problem is here?" I asked.

"I really don't know."

At this point in the confrontation, I didn't know what the problem was either. So I decided to explore a little. "Well, tell me this. What is your connection with your wife?"

"We don't have one, or much of one," he responded sadly.

"What is your wife's love language?" I asked.

"Encouraging words," he said, looking up at her.

His wife, sobbing, said, "In 18 years, he has hardly ever told me that he loves me."

We were finally onto something. I knew that this man was a passionate man. This man had been leading their ministry into great, anointed places. Their church had grown dramatically over the previous few years and was vibrant with life under this man's leadership. I asked him another question to help him see the contradiction he was living.

"Let me see if I understand what you are telling me. You lead people in the adoration and passionate pursuit of God's heart. You write songs that express this amazing passion and love for God. But you do not point any of this strength toward your wife. How about your kids?"

"I can't tell anybody that I love them, not even my kids," he said through tears. "I've turned out just like my father. My father cannot express love to anyone either."

We had just found the problem. This was the bottom of the barrel that no one outside of this family knew about or experienced. But we also had another problem. I didn't know what to do next. Then, all of a sudden, I got a word from the Lord.

I asked, "Are you trying to tell me that you can only love that which you think is perfect? Are you trying to tell me that you can only risk loving where there is no chance of failure? Are you telling me that you can only love what you believe to be perfect so there is no chance of getting hurt?"

His wife clearly got what I was asking, and fresh tears began to flow.

He started to shake his head, but then started to nod. Suddenly he said, "I have been deceived. This is the very thing I hated about my father. I've been deceived!"

I invited him to walk through a few minutes of forgiving his father. After he did that—wham!—He turned to his wife and said with complete sincerity, "I love you so much. I am so sorry!"

In a moment the whole room lit up. He kept confessing to his wife, "I love you. I love you. I didn't know what was wrong with me…"

As he said this, his wife's countenance changed completely. Hopelessness left the room as the woman began to experience that which, moments ago, she thought would only happen in Heaven. That is where they keep that stuff. We just had to go get some and bring it to Earth. In a few moments they were a couple of lovebirds, sitting there cooing.

Two miracles happened that morning. One was the gift of repentance that hit him and knocked him down. And the other one was her willingness to forgive him in a moment. The lights came on; he had a brand-new life and they had a brand-new marriage. He actually said, "I feel like the lights are on all of a sudden. I can see like I've never been able to see before. I feel like I am full of light!"

Simultaneously, we all remembered the word that Sheri had given him earlier in our time together. We talked and prayed with them some more, and Sheri prophesied over them again. It was a glorious time together with some wonderful people.

REFLECT

What was the real problem in this situation? What might have happened if the outward actions had been punished, but the heart issue was never addressed?

_____

_____

_____

_____

Through genuine repentance, this man experienced a heart change. How does this change affect the reality of his past sinful actions?

_____

_____

_____

Moments later he said, "You know, I'm not really sure I should feel this happy! I feel so hopeful. But I feel bad for feeling happy." A curious look crossed his face and he asked, "Well, now that I am a different man, what is my church's leadership going to do with me?"

That was a very good question. As wonderful a group as they are, I was pretty sure they would have a different perspective on the situation. The couple returned home, and I didn't hear back from them for a while. A few weeks later, my pastor friend called.

He said, "Danny! Hey, I'd like to ask you a few questions about the couple we sent up your way."

I said, "Sure."

"Oh, great!" he said. "We have you on the speakerphone right now at our elders' meeting. We are trying to figure out this situation. We heard some of the ideas you shared with them. We'd like to have you expound on those a little bit."

"Sure." My friend first shared some of the ideas that their board had been pondering. The basic plan was something like this:

- Inform the congregation of what was going on and have them pray for the restoration of these leaders.

- Have the couple step down for few months to work on their marriage.

- Review their progress after three to six months and, if favorable, slowly reintroduce them to the ministry.

REFLECT

What do you think of this plan? Does it seem reasonable to you? Why or why not?

_____

_____

_____

_____

This is the "Earth to Heaven" model that I know almost every church will attempt. It is Earth's best effort to rebuild trust and credibility for the people. It is designed to comfort the people first and address the life of the leader second. Whenever the anointing of the senior leader is primarily focused on people, the needs of the people rule the environment. This is the best method Earth can offer to bring about justice, fairness, or some other form of human comfort.

When the broken couple sat in my office a few weeks prior to this call, I had shared a "Heaven to Earth" model of handling this situation. I could hear that my pastor friend wanted to understand what I had shared with them. The unspoken explanation for his phone call was: *I think I understand what you shared with them. I want to come over to where you are. I want to address this from the light of Heaven and not the darkness of Earth's models. I am just not sure how to prove it scripturally.*

He said, "We would really like to get some input to help with our decision."

"Here is what I see," I began. "I see that for the past four years you've had a man who has led your congregation into the heart of God, and God has been pouring His blessing out on your congregation. More and more people have become attracted to the freedom that is growing in your environment. I see that in those four years you have birthed new ministries that are blessed and saturated with life and vigor. And the whole time, you have had a great, big, fat, lying, lowlife, dirtbag leader living a double life. You have given him raises, empowered him, and increased his influence more and more in your environment.

"Now what you have is a man who is in the best spiritual shape of his life. He went home from that week's vacation a changed man. He gathered his children, sat them down, looked into their eyes and said, 'Please forgive me. I have withheld my love for you your whole lives. I am so sorry. I *love* you. I *adore* you.' He showered love on his children for the first time in their lives and then invited them to speak up if at any point they feel that love dimming. Their whole household is filling up with light."

I went on, "This man has repented. He is a changed man. But, because you now know what has been hidden for the past four years, you think you have to punish him. If you do that, wouldn't it have been better if he had stayed a lying dirtbag, a prisoner of his bondage, for the benefit of your church? What are you going to do with the truth? This man doesn't need punishment, removal, a sabbatical, a vacation, a restraining order, or anything of that nature. This man needs some accountability to make sure he keeps the light on. And he needs to clean up his mess."

REFLECT

In what ways does the culture of punishment teach people that hidden bondage is better than coming into the light? What are the consequences of this?

_____

_____

_____

How would you suggest this man "clean up his mess"? Why?

_____

_____

_____

_____

They said, "Well that brings up another point. We were going to have him stand in front of the congregation and share what has happened with the church as an accountability measure. What do you think about that?"

I said, "Well, let me see if I understand this. As it stands, it's as if he had a gallon of paint, dropped it, got it all over your elder team, this other couple, you, and his wife and family. Now, you are going to give the man a 500-gallon bucket of paint and a grenade as a way to clean up his mess. I am all for people taking responsibility for their messes. I just don't understand why you would make a bigger mess than you already have. I think this mess is pretty easily cleaned up, and I think it is pretty easily repaired. That is what I think."

It was very quiet on the other end of that phone. One of them asked another question about something, and that was it. I said, "Bless you guys. I need to go."

Three months later at Bethel's Leader's Advance I met with my pastor friend and he said, "You would not believe how amazingly they are doing. His entire family looks like they have been raised from the dead. The light and the nourishment that have come to that home are breathtaking." He also said, "We handled the situation exactly as you suggested. It's awesome and it's working!" That happened in 2006, and they are all still getting stronger.

REFLECT

How do you feel about the outcome of this situation? Does it seem just?

_____

_____

_____

_____

_____

In what ways might you hesitate to apply this tactic to a situation in your life? What parts of this tactic cause you to feel anxious?

_____

_____

_____

_____

The devil is working to destroy us, and the "Earth to Heaven" model usually helps him accomplish his goal in the Church. I know that we are not trying to be destructive, but we are confined to our earthly limitations when our senior leaders are teachers, pastors, administrators, and evangelists who have not been hooked up to the flow of anointing and revelation in an apostolic government.

I am not a proponent of "keeping things in the family" as a way of handling destructive behaviors among Christians in the Church. If you throw the lights on and see that someone needs to go to jail, don't send a ministry team in to see the person instead. While I was the senior pastor in Weaverville, I reported five people in as many years to Child Protective Services and two of them were incarcerated. I have no problem involving the public authorities in situations when I know the Church can neither hold the people accountable nor supply them with the level of services necessary for them to get well. We must set clear boundaries, as Scripture teaches, for dealing with people who do not repent. But we must also learn to stop needing to punish people who _do_ repent. I'm not saying that we give them a "get out of jail free" card. But instead of punishing them and grinding them even deeper into the life of sin, we can call people to walk in their higher identity and responsibility as children of light.

When Heaven confronts us in our mistakes, it is like the Lord encountering Job and saying, _"Prepare yourself like a man…"_ (Job 38:3). Walking in the light is not for wimps. It requires a deep faith in God's love and in the power of His grace to provide what we need to change.

REFLECT

What is the difference between someone who has repented and someone who hasn't? Do you live like you believe this? In what ways?

_____

_____

_____

_____

A church's discipline culture is built to protect what people think—what they think about leaders and what they think about those who fail. When the comfort or expectations of people are held as the primary concern in the culture, and when the core belief of the people is that people who make mistakes are sinners, not sons and daughters, then discipline simply will not be administered in a Kingdom way. This is because the primary concern in a Kingdom culture is *"Your Kingdom come. Your will be done on earth as it is in heaven"* (Matt. 6:10).

Punishment's main purpose is to ease the anxiety of the people. We want to call it justice, but it is simply the fear of people demonstrated by leaders who feel the need to stay in favor with the people. As we saw in the lives of David and Peter, God's justice is baffling to human beings. We can only understand it when we give up trying to protect our relationship with the rules. When we start to protect a relationship with the law of life in Christ, our goal is never to assuage fear, but to restore broken relationships and to get life and love flowing again. Only one process will accomplish that: repentance. *We* have to lose our fear of sin and our fear of people, and *we* have to stop punishing those who repent.

It is for freedom that Jesus set us free (see Gal. 5:1 NASB). He has given us a way to stay away from the yoke of slavery to the rules; He offers us a way to protect our relationships— first with God and then with our families and those in our spheres of influence. Most important among those we influence are our children. They are the ones we impact most profoundly, and whatever we model, it is reflected clearly back to us by them. When our children no longer need to be punished for their sin, and when they learn that the priority when they fail is to restoring relationship (as opposed to accepting punishment), they will place a high value on relationships and will establish those relationships as the priority in the culture.[2] This is how we teach people to lead lives of love and liberty—and this is how we learn the power of trust and intimacy.

REFLECT

Why is punishment not the same as justice? In what ways does this contradict what you've believed or experienced?

_____

_____

_____

_____

TOOL: IDENTIFYING THE PROBLEM

1. **Ask: who is this person?** A key to identifying whether or not people believe a lie is to determine whether or not they see themselves as powerful and loved. As soon as power and/or love are "deleted" from a person's identity, he or she becomes a victim. Victims are responsible for nothing and, therefore, cannot change. They've given the power to change to something or someone else more powerful than them.

2. **Determine whether the person is willing to accept power and love.** Not everyone wants to be powerful, and therefore, not everyone wants to change or clean up his or her mess. Some people are successful in teaching the world around them that they are powerless and unable to deal with life. Although there are several good reasons why people learn to live this way, it doesn't change the fact that they are responsible for their lives and the consequences of their choices. Before you can move on with someone toward repentance, you need a person who is willing to become powerful and lovable. Without both in operation, the person will remain a victim of the situation and filled with anxiety.

3. **Help the person connect to love and power.** This is where the presence of God is so vital. Inviting the Spirit of God into the situation is the "game changer" for anyone who wants to move from being unloved to being fully loved. Simply invite God's presence into the room by asking, "God, will You come into this room with us right now and fill this place with Your love?" In a posture and mindset of receiving, allow the Lord to take over the environment. Again, another simple response is, "Thank You, Lord, for coming to be with us, and thank You for Your love."

4. **Begin to search for the problem.** In the presence of the Lord, there is freedom from the lies that invite destructive patterns into our lives. It's here that we begin to ask the Lord, "What lies am I believing about who I am in this situation?" The lies will bubble to the surface in a supernatural response from exposure to the light. God the Father is not interested in the person's punishment, but rather the person's freedom. It is here in this place of God's presence and love that we all get

to repent. We get to change or exchange what we have as a lie for what He gives us as the truth.

5. **Apply the truth.** There is no force that can resist the light. The greatest healing in our lives comes from the application of truth. If a person is experiencing pain, confusion, or depression, it will most likely trail back to some misalignment the person has with the truth. Once people discover the lies that are operating in their thinking, the next obvious step is to ask the Father, "What then is the truth You want me to believe about myself, my situation, or You?"[3]

TOOL: RESPONDING TO THE UNREPENTANT

1. First, you must understand the word and action of *repentance*. It can mean many things to as many different people. Usually it means to change one's course and to head in another direction. It also means to see things from a different vantage point or perspective. Regardless of your definition of *repentance,* it results in real change.

2. Choose to honor *before* you see change. Commonly, people want to see a lasting change before they honor. It is actually possible to do both at the same time. The fear of giving honor before it is earned is destructive. Therefore, you must have a commitment to make honor unconditional.

3. With these in place, you will be able to properly deal with the unrepentant. When people receive your honor, but do not supply the necessary repentance that cleans up messes and restores relationships:

   - Follow the steps in Chapter 1 Tools ("Questioning" and "Delegating the Problem-Solving in Love") to allow the opportunity for repentance.

   - Make sure the person understands that the goal is to restore relationships and bring about change so the problem doesn't reoccur.

   - Set limits on the person's future behavior.

   - Keep your honor on throughout this entire process—it is important.

   - Inform the person that he or she now has less access to the relationship, environment, or empowerment than previously. The degree of limitation and its severity is linked to the level of vulnerability of those affected by the "mess." The following are specific situations and corresponding courses of action:

- Illegal behavior, such as child abuse, domestic violence, stalking, or any situation involving the personal safety and protection from violence or injury: Call the police.

- Immorality, such as adultery, stealing, drug or alcohol issues, or other destructive behaviors that injure relationships: Establish boundaries that include statements such as "feel free to come back when you want a solution for your problems."

- Irresponsibility for job-related duties, commitments, roles, or common courtesy: Simply communicate the effects of this behavior on you and let the person know what you will do the next time this behavior shows up. Remember that although you do not control other people, you do have tremendous power over what *you* will do.

- Remember that you do not have a solution for anyone who does not have a problem. Do not work harder on someone's life than he or she does.

- Effectively remove other people's destructive cycles from your world as much as possible by setting limits. Hold your ground. Do not yield to threats or intimidation. Manage yourself no matter what other people do.

- Keep your honor on throughout this entire process.

DISCUSS

Discuss these questions with a friend or in a small group:

1. God is not afraid of your sin. How does this statement make you feel? What impact might it have in your life if you really believed it? If fear is no longer causing you to follow God, what will?

2. What does it mean to be a child of light? How has your identity changed? What impact does this have on your sin nature? Is this a reality in your life, or do you primarily see yourself as a sinner? How do you primarily see others?

3. When have you seen genuine repentance in action? How did it come about? What was the result?

APPLY

1. Study what the New Testament says about your new nature in Christ. (For starters, see Romans 8; Galatians 5 and 6; Ephesians 4:17-32; and Colossians 3:1-17.)[4] Write down and meditate on verses that particularly speak to you. Regularly ask God to renew your mind to comprehend your new identity and nature in Him.

2. Ask God to show you any instances in your life when you withdrew your love from (punished) another person who had offended you, even when that person was genuinely repentant. As He reveals these situations, ask Him how you can make restitution. Release these people from any further obligation or punishment. Instead, ask for God's help in seeing them the way He sees them. Write down what you hear, and use this list to renew your ability to see these people as children of light.

3. Consider what it means to not fear other people's mistakes. Try to find ways to practice this in small areas of your life. Ask: "What is the problem?' and "What are *you* going to do?" Journal about your results or tell a friend. This is a paradigm shift, so it will take work. Practice regularly.

ENDNOTES

1. See Matthew 26:34-35.

2. For more on parenting with honor, see my book *Loving Our Kids on Purpose* (Shippensburg, PA: Destiny Image Publishers, 2008).

3. For more on this, check out the Sozo materials by Dawna DeSilva and the Shabar materials by Teresa Liebscher at http://bethelsozo.com/.

4. The Crossing Church Website provides an excellent list of Scriptures that identify who we are in Christ: "Our Identity in Christ According to the Scriptures," Crossing Church, http://crossinglouisville.com/sermon/our-identity-in-christ/ (accessed December 21, 2011).

Chapter 5

FREEDOM PRACTICE—DEVELOPING A WEALTH MINDSET

After my oldest son, Levi, finished eighth grade at Bethel Christian School, he faced the question of where he would attend high school. Because he wanted to play football, he asked us if he could go to public high school. The biggest concern for us was the fact that at the public high school, Levi would be presented with freedom and options he'd never faced. He'd have to make successful decisions like never before.

First, we announced to Levi that this idea scared us. Then we reminded him of the extreme control freaks we could be when we were scared. Finally, we asked him how he planned to protect us through this proposed venture. Levi, realizing that he was a powerful participant in this decision, thought for a moment and said, "I'll be smart…and I won't break your hearts."

That was the right answer. And we believed him.

When game season began, the coach instructed the freshmen players to attend a varsity game. Levi came home and told us about the game, asking, "Can I go?"

When I looked at Sheri, I could see she was thinking the same thing I was thinking. We were both having flashbacks about what we had done at high school football games! We knew that we could not put any of our adolescent mistakes on him, but we were still scared of the possibilities that lay ahead in that Friday evening waiting to tempt him. So I said, "Son, we are very scared, but you can go."

"I can go!" he shouted. "Really? I can go? Awesome!"

I was certain that he hadn't heard me say that we were scared. He was too excited. I took him to the game and agreed to pick him up at 10 P.M. At that time, I drove back out to the field. There he was, right where he had said he would be. My heart was relieved. He jumped in the truck and told me all he'd learned that night—mostly how cool the varsity helmets and uniforms looked.

Later, as we headed into the house, Levi reached over, touched my arm, and said, "Dad, thanks for trusting me."

"You are welcome, Levi," I said. "Thank you for protecting us tonight, son."

REFLECT

Faced with this scenario, how might you have responded? What emotions or thoughts would have run through your mind?

_____

_____

_____

_____

How do you feel about the outcome of this story? Is it reproducible in your life? What can you learn from it?

_____

_____

_____

_____

THE POWER OF *US*

Levi knows that he carries tremendous responsibility in our relationship. He knows that no one can do his part of *us* but him. He feels the weight of *us* whenever he is out operating in his freedom. He knows that he is free to do whatever is in his heart to do. His heart is his to manage. And because it is in his heart to protect his relationship with his mom and dad, he makes decisions in consideration of how those decisions will affect us.

That is freedom training. Paul put it like this to the Corinthians: *"All things are lawful for me, but all things are not helpful..."* (1 Cor. 6:12). Freedom causes personal responsibility to rise to the surface. We either rise with it or lose our freedom. The only way to cultivate freedom is through learning how to handle an increasing number of options. Managing increasing options is how we expand our lives into ever-increasing abundance.

Jesus said that the thief is the one who came to steal, kill and destroy (see John 10:10). It's the devil who presents us with limitations; he's the one who removes our options and makes us afraid to live free lives. But Jesus came so that we *"may have life, and have it abundantly"* (John 10:10 NASB). Jesus has it in His heart to offer us a life of unlimited options.

Abundance, options, freedom, and choices—all of these describe a soul condition that we must master if we want a revival culture. It involves the development and expansion of a *wealth mindset;* this is an essential key to our success in bringing Heaven to Earth, and having it remain here. The practices of wealth are exercises in abundance. If we are to learn to steward the resources of Heaven, we must first learn to practice a wealth mentality.

REFLECT

Do you have a sense of your responsibility to maintain your half of us in your relationships with others? In what ways does this manifest or not manifest?

_____

_____

_____

_____

According to the definition of freedom mentioned, have you cultivated freedom in your own life and in the lives of others? In what ways?

_____

_____

_____

_____

How do you feel about your potential to live a life of unlimited options? What about the potential of others, like your spouse or children, to live this way? In what ways, if any, does this idea cause anxiety or fear within you?

99

_____

_____

_____

_____

WEALTH CREATES FREEDOM

The first mistake so many believers make when someone mentions wealth is to equate it to riches. But the idea that money makes someone wealthy is like suggesting that holding a football makes you an NFL quarterback. Riches or money are external conditions and wealth is an internal reality. Our insides will always manifest on our outsides.

For too many centuries, a religious fallacy has tried to rule the minds of believers and convince them that riches are the root of all evil. Thus, the poorer you are, the more spiritual you are. Somehow being a poor, weak, uneducated, lowly Christian is something God is cheering on in Heaven. Yeah, just like you are cheering your kids on to become welfare-dependent, high school dropouts. I am fully aware that in more recent decades, the American Church has swung to the other extreme and experimented with a "wealth gospel" that has led many to pursue powerful Cadillacs and comfortable lifestyles rather than powerful lifestyles and the Comforter. But a wealth mindset is not really about money or idolatry. It's about freedom.

REFLECT

Explain in your own words the difference between wealth and riches. In your mind, what epitomizes true wealth? Is this something you have personally experienced?

_____

_____

_____

GOD AND ABRAM

To help define a wealth mindset, I want to present you with a journey on which God led Abraham. Abraham started out with the name *Abram*. Eventually, he became *Abraham;* this happened as God moved him through a process in which the full measure of God's intended greatness was brought out in his life. When he began this process, Abram was already a rich man. He had many possessions and much land and was faithful in stewarding his wealth. He was a man whose outside already matched his inside. But in order to take him to the next level, God introduced a powerful set of instructions and steps that expanded Abram on the inside.

I want to challenge you to embrace this same process in your life; it will allow you to confront your own mindsets and the limitations you bring into your relationship with Heaven. It is so easy to limit your life in God, often because you do not see what hinders you.

In Genesis 12 we read of God's first interaction with Abram:

Now the Lord had said to Abram, "Get out of your country, from your family and from your father's house, to a land that I will show you. I will make you a great nation; I will bless you and make your name great; and you shall be a blessing. I will bless those who bless you, and I will curse him who curses you; and in you all the families of the earth shall be blessed" (Genesis 12:1-3).

God made it clear that He was going to transform Abram's life from something Abram thought was pretty good to something he could never have fathomed. In the New Testament, the apostle Paul tied us to this same promise. He wrote in Galatians that if you are in Christ, you are Abraham's seed and heirs to the promise that was given to Abraham (see Gal. 3:29). Through your life also, all the families of the earth shall be blessed. That is what you are carrying in your DNA. That is what you are carrying in your Father's name and in your identity as a child of the Most High God.

REFLECT

In what ways do you think you may have limited your life in God?

_____

_____

_____

_____

How do you typically think about your life vision and purpose—as meaningless, as pretty good, or as better than you can imagine? Why? What do you think God says about your destiny?

_____

FOUR KEYS TO NEW FREEDOM

There are four key aspects to the process that God began with Abram in Genesis 12. The first aspect is Abram's *name*. We focus on the fact that *Abraham* means "father of a multitude"[1] (or "*father of many nations*" as explained in Genesis 17:4-5). But it's important to see that *Abram* means "exalted father."[2] Abram was not just a regular guy. His very name reveals that he was willing to take on a higher position with more responsibility than the average father. Similarly, those of us who are taking strides to understand and carry the anointing and the revival that is happening today need to understand that God has asked us to take on a greater level of responsibility than the average person. Understanding this responsibility is what shapes us into people who are willing to follow God to a place "*whose builder and maker is God*" (Heb. 11:10).

REFLECT

In what ways is God asking you to take on a greater level of responsibility in helping to steward the move of God?

_____

_____

_____

_____

The second aspect of the process for Abram is the first thing God said to him. I want you to hear this as though God is saying it *to you*. He said, "*Abram, I want you to leave your country.*" In other words, God said, "I want you to leave your land. I want you to leave your territory, your geography. I want you to leave the limitations that you have come to accept as your container, your security, your realm of comfort and influence."

In any move of God, one of the recurring messages we hear is that God wants us to leave our comfort zones. We must have nothing but God to fall back on if we are going to tap into the wealth of Heaven. I recently heard Heidi Baker gently remind a North American audience that too many of us have a Plan B ready to go in case God doesn't show up. She pointed out that this alternate plan kills our hunger. It also stops up the heavens, because we end up channeling our resources to provide for personal comfort instead of channeling them toward Heaven's agendas.

The wealth mindset, the mindset that prepares us to participate in the flow of Heaven to Earth, is a mindset that embraces Christ's command to seek the Kingdom *first*, knowing that God will take care of our needs and desires (see Matt. 6:33).

REFLECT

Are you one who always has a Plan B ready in case God doesn't deliver? How might this be hindering your destiny?

_____

_____

_____

_____

In what way is God asking you to "leave your country" or step out of your comfort zone?

_____

_____

_____

_____

The third aspect of Abram's process was God's next statement: *"I want you to leave your family."* Interestingly, when Abram obeyed God, he took his family with him. What could God have been saying other than, "I am breaking up your family?" Family defines the circumstances of our birth. We gain identity from those we grow up with, and it's very difficult for that identity to shift and expand once it's been established in the perceptions of those around us.

You carry a particular identity in an environment filled with people who are very familiar to you. Whenever you are around them, they look at you in a way that says, "You will never escape the box that we have put you in." That identity may be a very comfortable box. You may be respected and admired by your family. But the reality is that only God, the One who designed you, understands your true identity and calling. In order to discover and become who He made you to be, you will need to go beyond the limits of what your family expects from you.

The Lord says to us, as He said to Abram, "I want you to leave your physical, geographical limitations, and I want you to leave your authority limitations. I want you to leave the territory that you have become comfortable in, and I want you to leave the identity that comes from the people who are most familiar with the person you have been."

REFLECT

What identity—good or bad—have you gained from your family and hometown environment? Do you believe this encapsulates your true calling and identity?

_____

_____

_____

_____

_____

What might God be asking you to do in order to leave behind the identity you've become comfortable with?

_____

_____

_____

_____

_____

Finally, He says to us, _"I want you to leave your father's house."_ Your "father's house" is the place where you receive your father's identity, your father's covering, and, in particular, your father's socioeconomic status. Your childhood environment placed you in a socioeconomic class, and this class has given you a lens through which you look at the world and the resources in your life. You naturally function within a particular class of people. You identify what is valuable, what is possible, and what different circumstances mean through the lens of your socioeconomic class.

Socioeconomic class usually comes with an accompaniment—a group of people who validate what you believe is true and what you see as being valuable. You are surrounded by people who see the world as you do. All of these people, along with numerous other cultural reinforcements of which you (and most of us) are mostly unaware, create your sense of "normal." There is usually no reason to think things are otherwise. All of us judge or make fun of the other classes and hold on to our own as though it were the one true class, the one true worldview. For most of us, our eyes have not yet been opened to the fact that there are more ways to see the world than the way we are currently seeing it.

What I want to present to you is something that I hope will open up your awareness to the way you see things now and the way your new identity (your true identity) is designed to see things. I hope to expose and confront your current viewpoint, because you are called to be a ruler. You are called to be a prince or a princess. You are royalty. You are wealthy beyond your wildest imagination. But unless you think like a wealthy person, you won't be able to handle your identity, role, responsibility, and resources.

REFLECT

What socioeconomic class did you grow up in? How do you generally view other classes?

_____

_____

_____

_____

CALLED TO BE RULERS

Proverbs 28:16 says: *"A ruler who lacks understanding is a great oppressor, but he who hates covetousness will prolong his days."* Literally, it means that a prince who does not see himself as a benefactor will punish others with his power; but one who hates gain by violence or controlling others will build a lasting legacy.

When a prince *thinks* like a pauper, he *lives* like a powerful survivalist, because the pauper learns one lesson in life, and that is how to stay alive. The socioeconomic worldview of the poor is completely governed by the fear of running out of their daily supply of resources. When you throw recording deals or professional sports contracts or winning lottery tickets at people who have been trained to survive, they become super-survivors. They have great resources, but they use them to protect themselves instead of to benefit others, because they believe that is what their resources are for. They see the world as something designed to serve them. What they don't realize is that, by misusing their resources, they are oppressing those around them. They destroy their own lives, and often the lives of those around them, because their worldviews were formed around how to survive, not how to thrive.

As believers, we are all in danger of being princes who think and live like paupers. Unless we are renewed in our thinking, we will not only abuse the great power and responsibility we've been given; we won't even be aware that we are doing so.

REFLECT

Which of these terms—survive or thrive—best describes how you view money? In what ways might this affect your self-perception as a child of God?

_____

_____

_____

_____

POVERTY, MIDDLE CLASS, AND WEALTHY

We are all constrained by the class view that we received in our "father's house." In order to understand these constraints and identify both how we think and how we should think, I am going to show you three socioeconomic class views: the view that looks through the lens of poverty, the view that looks through the lens of the middle class, and the view that looks through the lens of wealth. The class view you agree with the most is probably yours. My point here is not to debate what is right or wrong, but to give you the opportunity to see that, while you are now wealthy as a son or daughter of the King of kings, you might not be carrying a wealth lens through which to view your life.

Below is a chart that describes what each class values most in various aspects of life. After the chart, I will select a few of these topics and break them down to show you why we must "leave our father's house" and align ourselves with our new Father's House. (The chart is from a book entitled *A Framework for Understanding Poverty* by Dr. Ruby K. Payne.[3])

	POVERTY	MIDDLE CLASS	WEALTH
POSSESSIONS	People.	Things.	One-of-a-kind objects, legacies, pedigrees.
MONEY	To be used, spent.	To be managed.	To be conserved, invested.
PERSONALITY	Is for entertainment. Sense of humor is highly valued.	Is for acquisition and stability. Achievement is highly valued.	Is for connections. Financial, political, social connections are highly valued.
SOCIAL EMPHASIS	Social inclusion of people they like.	Emphasis is on self-governance and self-sufficiency.	Emphasis is on social exclusion.

	POVERTY	MIDDLE CLASS	WEALTH
FOOD	Key question: Did you have enough? Quantity important.	Key question: Did you like it? Quality important.	Key question: Was it presented well? Presentation important.
CLOTHING	Clothing valued for individual style and expression of personality.	Clothing valued for its quality and acceptance into norm of middle class. Label important.	Clothing valued for its artistic sense and expression. Designer important.
TIME	Present most important.	Future most important.	Traditions and history most important.
EDUCATION	Valued and revered as abstract but not as reality.	Crucial for climbing success ladder and making money.	Necessary tradition for making and maintaining connections.
DESTINY	Believes in fate. Cannot do much to mitigate chance.	Believes in choice. Can change future with good choices now.	Noblesse oblige.
LANGUAGE	Language is about survival.	Language is about negotiation.	Language is about networking.
FAMILY STRUCTURE	Tends to be matriarchal.	Tends to be matriarchal.	Depends on who has money.
WORLDVIEW	Local setting.	National setting.	International view.
LOVE	Conditional upon [being] liked.	Conditional upon achievement…	Conditional [upon] social standing and connections.
DRIVING FORCE	Survival, relationships, entertainment.	Work, achievement.	Financial, political, social connections.

REFLECT

What is your initial response to this chart? With which group do you most identify?

_____

_____

_____

_____

I'd like to zoom in on the topics of Food, Destiny, Worldview, and Driving Force in order to see the distinctions between these class perspectives more clearly and to see the influence of these perspectives on us as believers. Doing so will help us to recognize where we need to realign ourselves with Heaven.

	POVERTY	MIDDLE CLASS	WEALTH
FOOD	Quantity important.	Quality important.	Presentation important.

The way we relate to food indicates a lot about the way that we relate to all the resources by which we meet our basic needs. When we go to restaurants with a poverty mentality, we have certain expectations. We go because they give us tons of food. When the main concern is survival, our relationship with food is one of hoarding. We are operating from the belief that we are unsure when we will eat again. This belief doesn't have to correspond to reality for us to behave as though it does. With a belief system built on the priority of survival, we seek an experience that meets our need for quantity in regard to food. In other words: *buffet!*

When I cultivate the impulse to hoard, whether I'm hoarding food or something else, it prevents me from being generous to anyone but those whom I believe are worse off than I am. My waitress friends tell me that the Sunday afternoon crowd is the worst group to deal with—typically demanding, irritable, and stingy with their tips. Unfortunately, Christians with a poverty mentality go out for lunch after church and share their limited view of Heaven with their communities. We also often see a poverty mentality at work during offering time in church; the offering is accompanied by sad worship music and videos of tragic scenes that help people to feel more guilty about keeping their money than they feel afraid about giving it.

The middle class is more than free to eat whenever they want. Their resources give them many more options. Therefore, quantity is not a driving force in choosing what they eat. For the middle class, the value placed on food is determined by its quality. If it doesn't taste good, the middle class will pass. But if it's delicious, they will pay extra and come back later for more. They know they have the choice of where to spend their money, therefore, they had better get quality, in both food and service. If they don't, they simply will not patronize the eatery in the future.

This class view shows up commonly in how believers select their churches. The middle class realizes that they have options. They can attend any church in town. So, the quality of the experience had better be there or they won't be. They run the checklist: How was the teaching? Do they have a quality children's program? Were they friendly and helpful when we arrived? Do they realize that we can choose any church in town; therefore, it is their job to keep us and our money around this place? Do they know that we know people in this town?

REFLECT

In what ways have you approached your life in God through the lenses of hoarding or options, as described?

_____

_____

_____

_____

The wealthy are some "strange birds" to most of us. They can have all the highest quality food they could ever want. Therefore, they see food as a work of art, something worthy of the best *presentation*. Establishments serving food to the wealthy compete in how well-dressed their dishes are. These restaurants don't have cooks; they have artists and creative sculptors working in the kitchen. If a poor guy goes into a restaurant that serves the wealthy, he is shocked by the dainty portion that is covered by a bunch of "weeds." He is likely to be furious and think he is being ripped off when he discovers that this drizzle of a meal is costing him a week's salary.

Our class perspectives set us up to relate to resources in a certain way. If we have little, then we don't expect much more than getting our most basic needs met. But if we have more than enough, then we expect even the everyday experience of eating food to be an encounter with beauty.

Believers with a wealth-class view expect much more in their experience with God than salvation. While that is good and they are happy to be going to Heaven, these believers are very aware of what life on Earth is supposed to be like. They know there is more provision, beauty, power, and joy than they could ever exhaust, so they make sure that they are living in it every day, all day long. Anything less would be ridiculous.

REFLECT

Do you expect abundance in your experience with God? In what areas do you need to change your perspective? Explain.

_____

_____

_____

What, if anything, about this wealthy perspective makes you uncomfortable? Why?

	POVERTY	MIDDLE CLASS	WEALTH
DESTINY	Believes in fate. Cannot do much to mitigate chance.	Believes in choice. Can change future with good choices now.	Noblesse oblige.

Powerlessness is one of the primary effects of poverty. When people live in a resource-starved environment, they soon feel the very real constraints of limitation. Their lack of options makes them feel like victims—people whose lives are determined by more powerful external forces. As a result, they live superstitiously, believing that forces beyond their control are determining outcomes in their lives. They believe in fate, the idea that life is something that happens to them; they believe it is their job to do their best to adapt to whatever befalls them.

Destiny is an oppressive concept to the poor, because they believe that an external force has all the power. The poor are slaves of their lives; the corresponding feeling of powerlessness naturally creates anxiety and leads the poor to hang their hopes on a lucky turn of events. For them, life is about surviving within the context of their births. The young might hope to escape that context, but the hopes of their elders have been crushed by the cruel life of poverty. They may know a few gifted and "blessed" individuals who have escaped, but most are trapped by the same set of limitations that has kept them captive for generations.

When believers see their destinies in God through a poverty-class view, they live natural rather than supernatural lives. They find themselves trapped in natural problems with no apparent hope of heavenly intervention. They learn to blame God, labeling Him as the One who has the power to change their desperate situations, but chooses to do nothing. As they experience a powerless "gospel," they create a theology to sanction that experience; it is a theology where Heaven is a lot like Earth, God is a lot like them, and the outcomes of their lives are predetermined. Fate is called "God's will" and a life of limitation and powerlessness is called "humility" and "perseverance." The big "lottery ticket" for each generation is the Rapture. Since God is apparently not powerful enough or inclined enough to change their circumstances, the thing that gives them hope is the idea that He plans to rescue them out of those circumstances.

The concept of being powerful eludes those in a poverty class because life in God is not seen as a supernatural experience, but as more of what they have experienced so far.

REFLECT

In what ways does the previous paragraph describe your outlook on life and destiny? How has this feeling of powerlessness affected your vision for your life?

_____

_____

_____

_____

The middle class has a much more powerful interaction with life. They believe that their destinies and the quality of their lives are influenced by the fact that they have choices. Having options creates an expectation of freedom, and access to resources creates an expectation that one has power to change the environment by adding to it. When faced with problems, the middle class expects to be able to change a system or most limitations in order to move ahead with their desires. The middle class believes that dreams can come true. They believe that they can have anything they want if they continue in wise choices and moral, healthy practices. They believe it is their right to live free and they keep the power they need to preserve that freedom.

But the middle class also experiences limitations. There is a ceiling on the amount of money they have access to, and there are limitations to their power over their environments. Politics, media, and education are the realms of influence and power they turn to for help in improving their lives. Once these are exhausted, they seek solace in building something new in each of these arenas so that the next generation can strive for breakthrough. Whether it is a new political lobby, a new campaign, or a new area of expertise, they believe that building will lead them further along toward achievement and destiny.

The majority of American believers are caught in the middle-class view. We are known for our efforts to manipulate our environment. It is so tempting to try to make people think like us. After all, we love people, and we want the best for them. We want people to know Jesus and to have what we have. We want people to come to our churches, and we want the quality of our lives to be made available to everyone. We want our Gospel to fill the airwaves, to be taught in every school, and to be legislated from the highest places in the land. Perhaps the only thing that middle-class believers agree upon is this vision of the Gospel as a social and political panacea. The Christian Coalition as a political movement seemed like a great idea at the time and may still be one to some. Many of us would love to hear Rush Limbaugh, Oprah, or Bono say "God" or "Jesus" one more time.

REFLECT

In what ways do you live with the middle-class view of destiny and power in your Christian life? In what ways might this view have limited you?

_____

_____

_____

_____

The wealthy live in a limitless environment where there is no want. No one keeps them from getting whatever they set their hearts and minds upon. The wealthy are simply accustomed to getting their way. Whatever they ask for, they receive. This situation creates a mindset in them that few experience—a mindset of abundance. Living the reality of having more than you could ever use builds a sense of obligation within the life of the wealthy class. They see their role in life as one of *noblesse oblige*. This is the French term for the idea that people born into nobility or upper social classes must behave in an honorable and generous way toward those less privileged.

The wealth mindset is one of generosity. They see the favor and privilege of their lives as a responsibility to bring nourishment and strength to the environment around them. Destiny, to the wealthy, looks like pouring their lives into the long-term benefit of the society and genera-tion in which they live. They live to honor the momentum of their ancestors and to build on the family inheritance for their descendants. The wealthy understand that prosperity must expand if it is to last.

When we as believers begin to cultivate a wealthy-class worldview, we will see what apostles and prophets see. We will see and tap into the absolutely unlimited resources of Heaven. We will also see that these resources are an inheritance, something to which we have access because we have been grafted into the royal family line of God. This identity defines our responsibility to use these vast resources to benefit those around us. When we start to believe the limitlessness of what we have and the weight of what we are called to do with it, we will come to know and experience the reality of the promise that we will receive whatever we ask for. The supernatural will invade our lives, and we will finally lose the anxiety that has been so much a part of our Christian culture. We will leave behind the anxiety that naturally results from living a life devoid of personal experience with the realities that fill the pages of the Bible—the very realities we profess to believe and live.

Hopefully you can see how leaving our "father's house" and entering our new Father's House automatically takes our lives into a different realm of experience from the one in which our fathers lived. Though we appreciate and understand the legacy of those who have gone before us, we are not longing for the days of old. We are not praying that we would return to the "Book of Acts" Church or any prior Church era.

REFLECT

Why is longing for the "Book of Acts" Church detrimental to our growth?

_____

_____

_____

_____

In what ways have you lived, or not lived, with the sense of noblesse oblige as part of your Christian walk? What does this mindset look like in everyday life?

_____

_____

_____

_____

	POVERTY	MIDDLE CLASS	WEALTH
WORLDVIEW	Local setting.	National setting.	International view

All of us have a worldview. It is the scope and span with which we concern ourselves as we live our lives. The Internet and satellite television have helped to expand our consciousness of global affairs, but each class continues to focus on their own priorities in terms of worldview.

The poverty class sees life on the local level. Because resources are scarce, the poor cannot afford to be concerned with much that exists outside their immediate realms of responsibility. A neighborhood, a village, a town, or part of a city is the extent of concern and investment for the poverty mindset. Churches that have a poverty mentality see the world in the context of their congregations, their property, their denominations, and their missions programs. Their viewpoints are limited to those whom they can directly benefit or benefit from.

The middle class tends to be most concerned with their nation because they feel most affected by the condition of the national economic and political climate. Voting, national news, and economic forecasts are concerns they most readily take responsibility to invest in. Middle-class churches are the ones involved in "Get out and vote" campaigns and making sure that Christians know who the candidates are. Their prayer concerns are aimed at the social and political climate of the nation.

The wealthy class thinks internationally. Their lives are invested globally; therefore they are keenly aware of how activity around the world affects the global economy. The wealth mindset understands the "big picture"; the wealthy believe that global, national, and international communities must succeed.

Believers with a wealthy worldview travel and invest their lives in macro-influence. There's something about traveling to other nations, gathering with other believers, and seeing Heaven touch Earth during the ministry practice of miracles and healing that cultivates a limitless expectation in people's lives. It helps them to connect with the fact that the Gospel, the Church, and the Kingdom of God are global realities. It is a practical demonstration of the commission Christ gave us to *"go into all the world and preach the gospel to every creature"* (Mark 16:15). Worldview expands as we see how Heaven's agenda and resources are designed for global impact and how we have been called to partner in that global picture.

REFLECT

What worldview is most natural to you? What can you do to expand your perspective to see Heaven's global picture?

_____

_____

_____

_____

	POVERTY	MIDDLE CLASS	WEALTH
DRIVING FORCE	Survival, relationships, entertainment.	Work, achievement.	Financial, political, social connections.

What motivates you? Why do you get up in the morning? We see a variety of motivations in the classes. Each has its own set of core values that are based on the issues and priorities that propel its members through life. The driving force for each class is rooted in how they see the world they live in and how they relate to resources.

For the poverty class, the daily concern for survival creates the compass that directs decisions. Because their belief in their powerlessness is so strong, these decisions usually follow the path of least resistance, which supports the avoidance of pain. The quest for pleasure and escape begins each and every day, because life for the poverty class comes with too much pain built in.

To the poor, the value of relationships is found in the experience of love and social connection relationships offer. Family and good friends are the poor person's world; typically, family and friends spend a good portion of their lives together. Building relationships among neighbors is natural and even vital because these relationships often provide resource streams necessary for survival. Entertainment provides a fantastic method of escape from the harshness of the poverty reality. The ability to entertain others with skills, humor, or music catapults the individual to the most desirable places available to the poverty class. The value placed on entertainment and entertainers keeps this group producing both.

However, the strain of limited resources and the drive for survival usually lead to the erosion and abuse of relationships. Poverty negatively affects believers, too. When the driving force for believers is survival and escape from pain, they live in continual chaos. Divorce, rebellious teens, domestic violence, and financial upheaval are the culture of the home. Anxiety and fear threaten to devour anything that attempts to grow in these home environments.

Churches with this driving force struggle to create advancement and a growth environment; instead they tend to build a legacy of conflict and strife. Usually resources are the source of strife. As with many nations who spend decades in civil war, these churches are unable to recover from the last battle with the governing authorities among them. The tattered spoils of a formerly resourceful place tend to mark the remains of a church with a driving force of survival.

REFLECT

In what ways does this description apply to your family or church? Are there areas in your life in which survival and escape from pain are the motivating forces? Why?

_____

_____

_____

_____

_____

The ability to achieve is the driving force of the middle class, which explains why this group is often referred to as the "working class." Few things are as disgraceful or offensive to the middle class as those who do not work for a living. Working hard to support oneself is at the top of this class's value system because of the importance placed on possessions, planning for the future, and achievement. Education, personality, and even language are driven by the middle-class need to succeed by working one's way up the ladder of success.

In middle-class families, parents work to create opportunities for their children to get the kind of education that leads to well-paying jobs. Once children find such careers, the loop is complete. These middle-class children then work and become successful so they can send *their* children to good schools that will provide opportunities for well-paying jobs. Love is dispensed through this system. When children fail to complete the loop, parents struggle to feel like good parents and the family dynamic suffers a certain confusion and sometimes division.

Motivated by achievement, believers in the middle class have a "work gospel" that puts them to work for God. He has provided them with a "good education" in church and now expects them to be successful workers in His Kingdom. Therefore, the plans and goals of the middle-class Church are laced with works and achievement. According to the "works gospel," the more we achieve "for God," the more successful we are in ministry.

The middle-class Church also seems very businesslike; it empowers those who are either good businesspeople or high achievers. They typically rally around leaders who are also successful achievers. The rational sounds like this: "Dr. So-and-so is our leader because he has numerous credentials and has been endorsed by other high-achieving Christian leaders whom we all know and respect."

Without even trying, we end up with a so-called gospel of conditional love. It creeps into the environment because we are so busy celebrating the achievers in our midst that we don't see how poorly we treat those who are not "ringing the bell." Eventually everyone comes to understand that God loves us all, but *really* loves those who achieve. Unfortunately, this message in the Church is reinforced by the larger class culture.

REFLECT

In what ways have you embraced the middle-class "works gospel" that is focused on achieving? How do you feel toward those who don't achieve? How have you felt about yourself when you have failed to achieve?

_____

_____

_____

_____

As already mentioned, the driving force of the wealthy doesn't make much sense to the other classes. Each morning, they get out of bed to establish and strengthen their connections with other world-changers. The wealthy understand that there are a few powerful decision-makers who determine the global economic, social, and political climate. They see value in being connected to those decision-makers and they strive to get as close to them as they can.

The wealthy don't spend their lives working away at jobs. They are not training their children to get jobs. Instead, they send their kids to the schools where other powerful world-changers send their children. Connections are the driving force of the wealthy class. They believe that success comes, not from what you know, but from whom you know and who knows you.

Protecting and developing these relationships helps the wealthy to know what is going on all around the world. World leaders in politics, finance, and society choose to spend their time with one another for a reason: they recognize their power to direct the largest portion of the world's resources, and they work to protect their ruling-class momentum. They understand a way of life that other classes do not. They have experienced life without limitations and they know what kind of character and responsibility are needed to keep alive the freedom they enjoy, for their generation and the next. The wealthy do everything they can to teach their children to handle, protect, and pass on their secrets of limitless living.

REFLECT

What about this wealth mindset offends you or just fails to make sense? Why?

_____

Believers who embrace the priority and power of connections invest their time and energy to build relationships with other revivalists and train their children to do the same. They are willing to sacrifice to be where God's anointing is being poured out. They study and experience the works and wonders of God that are happening all over the globe. They are not satisfied to "work" for God, but will not stop until He pours His unlimited resources through their lives into the lives of others. Wealth-minded believers are melding their hearts with apostolic and prophetic leaders all over the world and directing their energy, resources, and time toward the success of these leaders. They know that in order for the knowledge of the glory of the Lord to cover the earth as the waters cover the sea,[4] the whole Church must be filled to overflowing.

The believer who carries a wealth mindset is one of the most important components in bringing Heaven to Earth. This mindset trains us to see our immediate circumstances from a limitless perspective; it also grounds us in our connections both to the global Body of Christ and to the generations behind and before us. It enables us to jettison the constraints of our past and create an inheritance for our children so that leaving their "father's house" for the Father's House isn't such a huge chasm to cross. Can you imagine how our children might live if they were trained from birth to walk in the limitless freedom of the Kingdom?

> *The believer who carries a wealth mindset is one of the most important components in bringing Heaven to Earth.*

REFLECT

What might it look like for you to embrace the wealth perspective as your driving force? How would you need to change your current approach to faith in order to embrace this perspective?

TOOL: STEPPING INTO A WEALTH PERSPECTIVE

1. **Honestly assess your worldview.** What, if anything, needs to change about the limitations placed on Heaven by your current expectations? If change is needed, assess which of the following questions best applies to your worldview: Are you moving from a mostly-poverty mindset to a middle-class one? Do you have some wealth paradigms mixed in with mostly middle-class views? Do you have mostly wealthy expectations, but find some areas in which a poverty or middle-class mindset remains strong? Take a look at those areas and ask, "Why?" Why are these areas posing a challenge to what you've come to expect from Heaven? What in your thinking needs to change before you will invite and allow *more of Heaven* to come into your life?

2. **Learn from "kings and queens."** Identify people (those you know personally or via Internet/media exposure) who have a wealth mentality (Bill Johnson and Heidi Baker are two who quickly come to mind). Sitting at the feet of such "kings and queens" will help you to learn how a wealth mentality serves to line you up with Heaven. This isn't about money, but about your capacity to receive greater abundance from the King of kings and His glorious Kingdom. Make sure you have people in your life who are challenging your ability to receive and grow. Persistently draw from people with a wealth paradigm (not from people who are living with the same mindset as you).

3. **Put forth challenges.** Once you identify the places in which you need to expand your capacity (move toward a wealth mindset), set goals to help you implement change in those areas. For example, what is your sense of destiny: is it a matter of fate, choices, or noblesse oblige? Do you feel caught up in the demands of your life, like you "have to do" this or that? Are you feeling powerless to change the realities and events of your life? Do you see yourself as being stuck with the cards you have been dealt by life or by God so that now you must endure and hope for your luck to change? Are you powerful in your choices, aware that the avenues for an improved life reside in the choices you make? Are you trying to improve your quality of life with better decisions? Do you carry a sense of responsibility for the world around you? Knowing that you are living a blessed and favored life, do you have a plan to nourish the society around you with the strength, resources, and access to Heaven that you enjoy as a believer?

4. **Be accountable to grow.** Identify people in your life who can provide feedback about your personal assessment. If you do not have anyone like this, consider what you need to do to begin cultivating these types of relationships. Will you allow

someone to tell you what he or she sees about your wealth paradigm? Write down your goals for growth, including start dates and review dates. Share these goals with someone who will believe with you, yet speak honestly into your growth process. Write down the desired results of your goal—in other words, how will you know when you have accomplished your desired changes?

DISCUSS

Discuss these questions with a friend or in a small group:

1. In what ways have you experienced or not experienced freedom (as described in this chapter) in your life? What steps do you think God may be inviting you to take in order to embrace your "freedom training"?

2. In what ways have the poverty and middle-class mindsets in these four areas— food (provision), destiny, worldview, and driving force—played a part in your life and church? What can you do to break free from any limiting perspectives?

3. What are your thoughts on the Kingdom wealth perspective shared in this chapter? What parts of it resonate with you? What parts are you struggling to understand or accept? How do you feel about the idea of living life this way?

APPLY

1. Do you think of yourself as a prince or a pauper? Take Kris Vallotton's Prince & Pauper Test at http://www.kvministries.com/prince-pauper-test. Pray about the results, asking God to renew your mind to see yourself the way He sees you.

2. Looking at the four keys to freedom in Abraham's life, ask God what He wants to do in each of these areas in your life. Write down what you hear and share it with a trustworthy friend. Then be obedient and step out in faith, believing God is preparing you for the greatness of your destiny in Him.

3. Using the chart from this chapter, study at least three of the categories not discussed in depth. Write about how these perspectives affect believers and their approaches to life in Christ. Consider how these perspectives have influenced you as well. Ask God to renew your mind and to give you the practical steps you can take toward a wealth perspective.

ENDNOTES

1. Biblesoft's New Exhaustive Strong's Numbers and Concordance with Expanded Greek-Hebrew Dictionary, CD-ROM, Biblesoft, Inc. and International Bible Translators, Inc. (1994, 2003, 2006) s.v. "Abraham," (OT 85).

2. *Blue Letter Bible*, Dictionary and Word Search for *"Abram"* (Strong's 87), 1996-2011, <http://www.blueletterbible.org/search/translationResults.cfm?Criteria=Holy +Spirit&t=KJV> (accessed January 7, 2012).

3. Ruby K. Payne, PhD, *A Framework for Understanding Poverty*, 3rd ed. (Highlands, TX: aha! Process, Inc., 2003), 59.

4. See Isaiah 11:9; Habakkuk 2:14.

Chapter 6

THE TOP PRIORITY OF LEADERSHIP

Thomas Jefferson is credited with saying, "Free people are the most difficult to lead." Unfortunately, many church leaders have not mastered the difficulties of leading free people. In order to lead free people, we must establish environments in which they can gain freedom and governments by which they can keep it. Generally, classic church environments are known for neither. Those who come in are usually ready to give up whatever they have to in order to get free from their pain. When these people learn that God is a master who wants to control them (as many do) it makes me suspect that church leaders do not understand our Gospel of freedom. A controlling God, who is usually represented by a controlling church leadership, cannot be called "good news."

In order to lead free people, we must establish environments in which they can gain freedom and governments by which they can keep it.

How can church leadership create freedom and not more rules? How can we bring out the best in human beings and keep their best in sight even as we deal with their problems and short-comings? Can we empower others and release them to live from their best natures and from the truest reasons they are alive? Will we as Christian leaders, parents, and employers take on the responsibility to become proficient at drawing out the dreams and destinies of the people we lead?

REFLECT

How do you feel about the idea that people in the Church should be free? What does this look like to you? As a practical matter, does it seem feasible, or is it just a nice (but unworkable) idea? Why?

_____

_____

_____

_____

Let me show you an example of what leading free people might look like. My daughter Brittney was 14 once. And like most 14-year-olds, her idea of getting the dishes done was completely different from my wife Sheri's. For this reason, I often heard conversations that sounded something like this:

Sheri would say, "Britt, time to do the dishes."

And Britt would reply, "I will, in just a minute."

That minute would turn into 20, and Sheri would fire off another, "Britt, it is time to get those dishes done."

Britt would volley back with, "I am doing my homework like you said!" or "I am on the phone! I'll be done in just a minute."

This was part of our evening ritual for several months. Numerous times, Britt made the verbal commitment to finish the dishes, only to fail and have my wife wake up to dirty dishes in the morning. There are several things that my wife does not like in this life: injustice, sushi, bugs, scary movies, and _waking up_ to dirty dishes!

Finally, it happened for the last time. Britt went to bed late on a Friday night and forgot to wash the dishes. On Saturday morning, shortly after Sheri discovered the pile of dirty dishes, she and Britt had a little conversation about them. I could hear their "little conversation" at the other end of the house. Once finished with Brittney, Sheri came to tell me what had happened. I told her that I had already heard. Meanwhile, Brittney's friend, Rebecca, came over and was visiting Britt in her room. When Sheri and I came looking for Britt to discuss the dish situation, we discovered that, unannounced, Britt and Rebecca had left our house and gone down the street to Rebecca's house. Sheri looked at me with fire in her eyes. Suddenly, it appeared as though her head burst into flames, her skull split open, and a dragon came out of the top.

The dragon looked at me and said, "What are _you_ going to do?"

"Me?" I replied, suppressing a smile.

"Yes!" the dragon said. "What are you going to do about *your* daughter?"

"Now you want *me* to deal with this situation? Is that what you are saying?"

"Yes!" the dragon said, breathing fire.

REFLECT

What would you do in this situation?

_____

_____

_____

_____

I ran in and did the dishes.

Now, "doing the dishes" at our house involved moving the dishes from the sink into the dishwasher. That was all I did. It maybe took me six minutes. Maybe.

Brittney and Rebecca came back to our house all dolled up with makeup and matching ponytails. Britt asked, "Mom, Dad, can I go to the mall with Rebecca and her mom?"

I thought we would all get to see the dragon again, but instead Sheri was biting the side of her hand, a sign that I was to handle the whole intervention. I said, "Brittney, sweetie. I did the dishes for you."

She said, "Dad, that is not fair! I was going to do them! *Ugh!*" Britt began to do little jumps that never actually got her feet off the ground, but were intended to communicate that she did not like what was happening.

Rebecca watched this exchange with a confused look on her face. She finally asked Britt, "Are you in trouble? How do you even know you are in trouble? Nobody is even yelling."

Brittney said, "He's going to trade me chores!"

"Sweetie, which chore would you like to trade me? Would you like to do the trash shed for me or the chicken coop?"

"Ugh! Well, can I look?"

"Of course you can! Of course you can choose which one you are going to do." And thus I empowered the child. I wanted her to feel powerful around me.

Out she went.

For those who might not know, the trash shed is a Weaverville cultural experience. Garbage cans left outside would end up with dogs, cats, or raccoons in them, so we had to put the trash in an enclosed area. The door on the shed had a window in it, and once I saw the trash bags through the window, I knew it was time to go to the dump. It was a big old hassle, so I was always waiting for one of my kids to trade me chores.

Britt went and opened the door to the shed. Ten million flies swarmed out and buzzed around her face. "Gross!"

Rebecca nearly started running backward, yelling, "What the heck are we doing out here?"

Brittney spat out a fly and rolled her eyes. Then she headed toward the chicken pen. By the time she got there she was pretty angry and kicked at the chickens as she entered. "Stupid chickens!"

She opened the chicken coop and was completely grossed out by the stench. Then she came back into the house and said to me, "Chicken pen."

"Awesome, Britt! Thank you!" I replied, excited that I wouldn't have to do that chore this time. Then I asked, "Now, would you like to do that today or tomorrow after church?"

"I can do it tomorrow? Really? Can I go to the mall today with Rebecca?"

"Sure, if you want."

"I can! Oh, Daddy! Thank you! Thank you!"

REFLECT

How did this exchange make Britt feel powerful? Do you tend to use anger or control (consciously or subconsciously) to try to determine the outcome of a situation?

_____

_____

_____

_____

How do you feel about the fairness of the situation? Would you have let Britt go to the mall and postpone her consequences? Why or why not?

_____

_____

_____

You may be thinking, "What? You let a transgressor go? You let a sinner escape the due punishment she had coming? Your child got to have freedom and privilege without first experiencing the suffering that would have taught her a lesson? Don't you know that there is need for the shedding of blood for the atoning of sin? How will this child ever learn her lessons?"

Hang on. The story isn't over.

So, off they went to the mall and had a great time. The next morning we went to church, and by the time we got back, it was pouring rain. Why? Because Jesus loves me! Meanwhile, Brittney was trying to be invisible.

I said to her, "Hey Britt, sweetie! Would you like to wear my rubber boots or those pretty little slippers you've got on there?"

"Your rubber boots."

"Do you want to wear my rain jacket or that pretty sweater you have on?"

"Your rain jacket."

"Do you want to use the pitchfork or the shovel?"

"I'll probably need both."

Off she went. One…two…*three* hours later, Brittney came in, dragging the shovel and the pitchfork. She had straw hanging off her sopping wet head. I met her at the back door and asked her what she needed.

She said, "I'm done."

"Awesome! Thank you very much."

"Whatever!" Off she went to take a shower.

Sometime later that week, I heard Sheri say, "Brittney, get those dishes done."

Then I heard Brittney say, "Ugh. I will in just a minute."

So I got up and said, "Britt, I got them for you!"

Just as I got off the couch, she came *flying* through the house, yelling, *"You get away from my dishes!"*

I smiled and said, "Hey, I'm just trying to be helpful. But, if you ever need me to do your work for you, I'm your man."

There is a way to lead people into freedom in such a way that personal responsibility rises to the surface. It requires us to trust people. But it never ceases to amaze me how, when we trust

people to rise up and see the wisdom in their choices, we get to see them become greater people in our relationships with them. People want to be trusted and they want to be free.

REFLECT

What do you think of the outcome of this story? How were personal responsibility and freedom taught?

_____

_____

_____

_____

Do people usually feel free and powerful around you? Why or why not? What can you learn from this example?

_____

_____

_____

_____

CREATE A SAFE PLACE

Why do you suppose free people are so difficult to lead? The problem of leading free people is connected to a question about the universe that philosophers and theologians have worked on for centuries. It's connected to the fact that God, the leader of the universe, created us to be free. In fact, God *trusted* us with freedom. In *Mere Christianity*, C.S. Lewis presented a concise account of the situation:

> God created things which had free will. That means creatures which can go either wrong or right. Some people think they can imagine a creature which was free but had no possibility of going wrong; I cannot. If a thing is free to be good it is also free to be bad. And free will is what has made evil possible. Why, then, did God give them free will? Because free will, though it makes evil possible, is also the only thing that makes possible any love or goodness or joy worth having. A world of automata—of creatures that worked like machines—would hardly be worth creating. The happiness which God

designs for His higher creatures is the happiness of being freely, voluntarily united to Him and to each other in an ecstasy of love and delight compared with which the most rapturous love between a man and a woman on this earth is mere milk and water. And for that they must be free.

Of course God knew what would happen if they used their freedom the wrong way: apparently He thought it worth the risk.[1]

The difficulty in leading free people is *risk*—the risk that they could use their freedom the wrong way. But unlike God, many of us in the Church do not understand why the risk is worth it. The threat of misused freedom looms larger than the prize of true freedom. And because of that, we get scared. In the United States, the supposed leader of the free world, fear is rampant. We as believers need to tap into some pretty powerful stuff if we are going to resist the fear in our culture and extend trust to God and people. We also need to pound into our belief system Heaven's value for freedom.

REFLECT

How do you feel about the risk that people will use their freedom wrongly? In what ways has fear dictated your responses to people?

_____

_____

_____

_____

As Lewis pointed out, the whole value and purpose of freedom is love. When we use our freedom to love, as He intended us to do, our freedom and the freedom of those around us are protected and cultivated.

As leaders, we need to accomplish many things, from defining reality to reaching productive goals. But, the priority of Heaven is crystal clear: "If you have not love…you're just noisy."[2] Leaders who extinguish love in the process of reaching goals have achieved Earth's priorities, maybe. But, the higher goals of Heaven require us to cultivate and preserve love, and thus freedom; for you cannot have love without freedom. God is love, and His Kingdom is a Kingdom of freedom. This is why the Bible tells us, *"The Lord is the Spirit, and where the Spirit of the Lord is, there is freedom"* (2 Cor. 3:17 NIV). This verse is saying that when God shows up, people feel free. If that is not happening, we should wonder why. Why isn't freedom breaking out in more places? Could it be because a lot of people, including leaders, misunderstand the goal of God's leadership in our lives?

> *I propose that the goal of God's leadership in our lives and,*
> *consequently, the goal of church leaders, is to create a **safe place***
> *in which to discover who we are and why we are here.*

I propose that the goal of God's leadership in our lives and, consequently, the goal of church leaders, is to create a *safe place* in which to discover who we are and why we are here. A safe place is one in which the fear of misused freedom isn't allowed to rise up and intimidate us out of risking trust and love in our relationships with one another. A safe place is what gets cultivated when freedom is expressed through love. The essence of love is *safety* and *connection*. If people don't feel safe to be themselves and don't feel a sense of connection with those around them, then it's hard to convince them that they are in a loving place.

FEAR VS HONOR

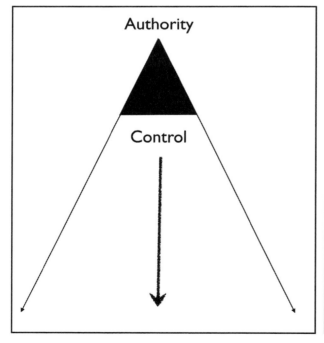

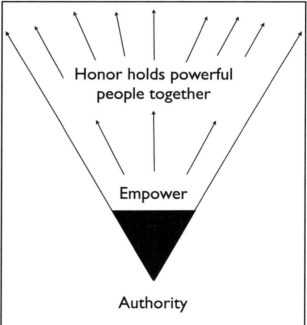

REFLECT

How are freedom and love connected? In what ways have you experienced this connection in your life? Which have you generally valued more: freedom or productivity? What has been the result?

_____

_____

_____

_____

When have you created a safe place for others to discover their identities and purpose? What were the results? What usually holds you back from being a safe place for others?

_____

_____

_____

_____

If the essence of love is safety and connection, would you say that most of your relationships are characterized by love or by fear and performance? Why?

_____

_____

_____

_____

Now, we won't step into the experience of a safe place with God and His people until we understand and believe that it's what God wants for us. My experience is that most people, including Christians, think God wants us to line up, stay in line, and be good. We've embraced the idea that He is patient, yet on the verge of anger. For most people, God is a scary character—unpredictable and strict. But consider what God said through the prophet Isaiah: _"The mountains may be removed and the hills may shake, but My lovingkindness will not be removed from you, and My covenant of peace will not be shaken..."_ (Isa. 54:10 NASB).

The mountains and the hills are going to be taken away? Can you imagine watching a mountain being taken away? Can you imagine what would be required for that to happen? It would require more than a little violence and would be pretty scary. God is saying that He is not unpredictable. He wants us to be completely sure of His attitude toward us: "My kindness and My covenant of peace will never be taken away." God wants us to have a blessed assurance, a truth that positions us to look for the freedom that comes to us when Jesus shows up. This mentality, this expectation, and this security allow us to be free everywhere we go.

No matter what case you make against God, no matter which Scriptures you use to make it, no matter what you do to build a different reality—His kindness and His peace will never be taken from you. That word *peace* is literally the Hebrew word *shalom*. From this word we get several powerful definitions. Here's Strong's definition:

> **shalowm**…or **shalom**…safe, i.e. (figuratively) well, happy, friendly; also (abstractly) welfare, i.e. health, prosperity, peace: …do, familiar, fare, favour, friend, great, (good) health, (…such as be at) peace (-able, -ably), prosper (-ity, -ous), rest, safe (-ty), salute, welfare, (…all is, be) well, wholly.[3]

Please notice that the first definition of *shalom* is "safe." Our covenant with God is a *safe place*. The power in this reality is this: as human beings, we blossom in safety. This is why *shalom* also means "health" and "wholeness." The nourishing effects of His presence stimulate the deepest parts of the best in us. This is why He says that His covenant is for our welfare and not our calamity (see Jer. 29:11 NASB). His covenant brings peace, happiness, safety and completeness, and it will never be taken from us. When He shows up, His presence is a safe place.

REFLECT

Have you typically viewed God as being a safe place, predictably kind and loving? Or have you more often viewed Him as strict and unpredictable? How has this affected your relationship with Him?

_____

_____

_____

_____

When the Lord shows up, His atmosphere is charged with *shalom*. He brings a safe place everywhere He goes. It never ceases to amaze me how many people want to make the unfounded case that God is scary, but they do. This is why we as leaders at Bethel understand that one of our primary jobs is to declare on a regular basis God's true nature and attitude toward us. Almost every time we do it, we can feel it directly confronting the wrong thinking in the room. So many times I've heard Bill Johnson declare to a congregation that God is in a good mood, only to hear nervous laughter break out all over the place, as if to say, "He-he. I have never thought of God like that before."

I myself have made the same statement in places where I've spoken. "God's in a good mood!" I can see the confusion in some people's eyes. It is as though they want to pick up their Old Testament and yell out, "Not in this part of the Bible He's not."

Yes, He is! He is in a good mood, from start to finish, and you can make a case for that, too.

REFLECT

Do you agree that God is in a good mood? What, if anything, bothers you about this statement? Why?

_____

_____

_____

_____

This truth would seem to be a no-brainer since Jesus came and introduced a New Covenant. God is very familiar with His original design for us to need a safe place. The Garden of Eden was such a place. We are at our best when we are safe, when we are happy, when we feel whole, and when we have peace. When our peace or safety is disrupted, our physical bodies begin a process of shutting down our best and preparing us to show our worst.

It works something like this: God put this little gland inside our brains called the amygdala. It is an almond-shaped mass of nuclei located deep within the temporal lobes of the brain. This gland is important for determining emotional responses, especially those associated with fear. For example, if somebody is "not safe" or does something explicitly threatening or unexpected in your environment, your amygdala kicks on and begins to flood your body with one of more of the following messages: _React! Defend! Disappear! Fight! Flee!_

These are some of the responses in which we show our worst. It doesn't take a rocket scientist to discover that people who are scared are not at their creative best. Scared people are not thinking about the team, family, church, or anyone else beside themselves. Fear is a dangerous emotion for humans to navigate. Most do not manage it well.

REFLECT

Think of a time when you responded in fear. What impact did it have on your environment and the people around you?

_____

_____

_____

_____

As you can see, when we do not feel safe, we are likely to become dangerous ourselves, because fear is directing our behavior. Imagine what happens when the *leader* in a given environment is directed by fear. A majority of leaders—not just Christian leaders—are pretty uptight. The same goes for far too many parents. If there is something important going on and the outcome matters to you, there is a good chance you are going to bring *uptight* with you.

Of course, another word for *uptight* (or stress or anxiety) is *fear*. And here's the thing—when we are afraid on the inside, there is more than a good chance we are spreading that fear to those outside of us. Whether or not we are believers, we are creative and spiritual in nature. We are spiritual conductors; each of us creates an atmosphere (a reality or a *spirit*, if you will) around us. But we can only reproduce on the outside that which is already on the inside. When our thoughts and affections are wrapped up with a spirit of fear, we might think we are smoothly hiding it, but we cannot mask it. The anxiety we allow to operate in our lives *will* come to the surface.

REFLECT

Are you often uptight? In what ways do you see uptight showing up in the people around you?

_____

_____

_____

_____

Unfortunately, too many people become accustomed to living in an environment where the people in charge are uptight. Most of us are trained early in life that people who are in charge are unsafe and can hurt us. Sometimes we learn that powerful people *will* hurt us. From our earliest childhood experiences to our most recent run-ins with authority figures, we build concepts about what we can expect from leaders and from God, our ultimate authority figure. If fear is what we have learned, imagine what our amygdalas are doing the entire time we are in the presence of powerful people! What is the impact to our potential in God? How will we ever become whole, free, or healthy under those conditions?

The answer is simply that we won't. But the good news is that the conditions are changing. Heaven, the Kingdom of love and freedom, is invading Earth, and love is directly confronting the fear that has governed us. Fear and love are enemies. These two spirits will not occupy the same place. Love and fear are like light and dark, fresh water and salt water, blessing and cursing. One of them has to win. Scripture reveals that love casts out fear (see 1 John 4:18). Love not only casts out fear, but also brings security and safety and *shalom*. This is the fruit I am seeing in an apostolic environment. Fear is leaving people's lives. Freedom is growing in worship and in our relationships with one another as people are starting to get it: He is a safe place.

REFLECT

What has life experience taught you to expect from authority figures? How has this shaped your view of God?

_____

_____

_____

_____

Have you ever experienced love overcoming fear? Explain. What impact did it have on you?

_____

_____

_____

_____

What needs to happen in your heart for you to become a conduit of love (and not fear) in people's lives?

_____

_____

_____

_____

As I indicated in the first chapter, creating a safe place is the essential condition for a revival culture. The fact that miracles, signs, and wonders have not only happened in our midst, but have continued to happen for years now, points to the fact that something has been established—a wineskin of healthy people and relationships that manifest and carry the *shalom* of Heaven.

As I explained in the second chapter, there is an order for leadership, a structure that sustains the flow of the heavenly reality of grace in people's lives. This structure also facilitates the core values and truths that an apostolic leadership holds dear. It is not a small thing that our leader regularly declares the goodness of God over us. If leaders believe that God is good and in a good mood, then the people will follow and learn for themselves that this is true. If leaders understand that their top priority is making the house of God a safe place, the people will encounter this safe place of God's covenant in their lives. As their anointings, potential, and creativity rise to the surface, there will be room to manifest those things in the Church.

When leaders create environments in which people can feel loved, safe, and free to be themselves, we will change the world with the Kingdom of Heaven!

REFLECT

Have you experienced this kind of leadership in your life? What can you do to be this kind of leader in your sphere of influence?

_____

_____

_____

_____

HONOR AND CONFLICT

One of the most vital core values in creating a safe place for people to be free is *honor*. Honor is the relational tool that protects the value people place on those who are different from them. Free people cannot live together without honor. Conversely, honor can be successfully applied *only* among powerful people possessed of a true sense of their personal responsibility to preserve the freedom around them. We *must* be free to be ourselves in this life and in the communities we share.

High levels of freedom can generate conflict. This friction usually occurs because others live in ways that flood our amygdalas. Without the core value of honor, our discomfort with those who choose to live differently from us tempts us to shut down their freedom. Obviously, when I speak of different ways to live, I am not suggesting that immorality or violations of our relationship with God are viable options for anyone. But many Christians disagree about how to live. When people begin to walk in freedom, they will say and do things that demonstrate their belief that conformity is not a priority. This approach clashes with much of our Christian-culture experience. I am not building a case for people to be rude, uncaring, or obnoxious, but I am trying to point out that free people are not terribly interested in putting on façades. When we believe that the people around us are not protecting our paradigms, our amygdalas get jacked up. This is how we often end up showing others our worst.

The culture of honor both facilitates a safe place *and* creates a place of great conflict. The question is whether we will learn to use honor to navigate conflict when it arises. Conflict is not inherently evil. As a matter of fact, when conflict goes away, it is a sign that *life* probably left with it. We are quick to hope that peace will bring the absence of conflict. In reality, true peace is always the result of victory. I cannot think of a single victory that did not begin with a struggle.

REFLECT

How do you usually respond to conflict? How do you feel when other people's values or beliefs differ from yours? What effects does this "mismatch" have in your life?

_____

_____

_____

_____

TOOL: CREATING A SAFE PLACE

1. Acceptance. A key to helping people feel safe is *meeting needs*. People need a place where they can be themselves. The way you ensure this safety is by staying aware of the feelings you experience when people stop reminding you of *you*. How do you respond when people say things, do things, or behave in ways that you wouldn't? Here are some hints for ensuring safety:

- Don't be the judge.

- Look for the value in others.

- Communicate your love first, and then your thoughts.

2. Freedom. Another aspect of creating a safe place is learning *not* to grab for control in a situation. People who feel controlled do not feel safe. Like all people who feel scared, we want control. Remember and become more aware of this human tendency. Create the habit of telling people what you plan to do, and get out of the pattern of barking out commands when you feel scared or uncomfortable. You can avert control-grabbing by:

- Asking good questions.

- Allowing the other person to think and problem-solve in front of you.

- Resisting the temptation to solve all the problems for the people you care about.

3. Validation. The need for validation is strongest in a disagreement, yet we tend to reduce the value of people with whom we disagree. This tendency shows up as soon as we realize that someone has to be wrong. In fear, we try to protect ourselves by making sure *we* are not wrong. The Heaven-to-Earth model is to validate others in the midst of conflict. This creates a safe place for them, and enables them to share from their hearts. Here are some keys to validation:

- Listen well.

- Ask clarifying questions.

- Make understanding the goal of your communication, instead of agreement.

DISCUSS

Discuss these questions with a friend or in a small group:

1. What does it mean to be free and powerful? Have you encountered people like this? How did you feel around them? Do you live as a free and powerful person? What can you do to make this more of a reality in your life?

2. Think of a time when someone used their freedom wrongly and hurt you in the process. How did this make you feel? What fears do you have as a result? What can you do to allow God to free you from these fears?

3. What is your experience with authority? In what ways have you, or haven't you, experienced godly leadership in your life (as described in this chapter)? How has that influenced your view of God?

APPLY

1. In reflecting on the story about Britt and the dishes, imagine scenarios in which you are confronted with the desire to control people in order to protect yourself from their mistakes. Imagine and practice responding in ways that teach them responsibility through freedom. Practice these responses on the people in your life.

2. Do a study of the word *peace (shalom)*. From the study, describe God's character as revealed in the Bible. Write down and meditate on the truths about His nature and the reality that He is a safe place for you. Ask Him to make these truths real in your heart so that you can relate to Him in confident love rather than fear. Regularly pray: "Thank You, God, for being a safe place for me."

3. Think of someone who has different values or beliefs from yours (not sinful, just different). In what ways have you responded to these differences: in fear or in love? Ask God to help you honestly examine your heart, and ask Him to show you how to fully embrace this person, despite the differences in belief or values. If necessary, apologize to this person for allowing your fear to cause you to respond in unloving ways.

ENDNOTES

1. C.S. Lewis, *Mere Christianity*, (New York: HarperCollins, 2001), 47-48.

2. My paraphrase of First Corinthians 13:1.

3. Biblesoft's New Exhaustive Strong's Numbers and Concordance with Expanded Greek-Hebrew Dictionary, CD-ROM, Biblesoft, Inc. and International Bible Translators, Inc. (1994, 2003, 2006) s.v. "shalowm" or "shalom" (OT 7965).

Chapter 7

KINGDOM CONFRONTATION

There will be no culture of honor without the active use of effective confrontation. The skill of combining these two relational elements—honor and confrontation—is the key to sustaining an environment of grace.

Paul wrote to the Galatians extensively about the fact that we are a people called to walk in freedom and love through the internal government of the Spirit of God. This idea is not new; it just seems that we, like the Galatians, have a difficult time catching on to it. Let's review Paul's description of us as mature heirs:

> *Now I say that the heir, as long as he is a child, does not differ at all from a slave, though he is master of all, but is under guardians and stewards until the time appointed by the father. Even so we, when we were children, were in bondage under the elements of the world. But when the fullness of the time had come, God sent forth His Son, born of a woman, born under the law, to redeem those who were under the law, that we might receive the adoption as sons. And because you are sons, God has sent forth the Spirit of His Son into your hearts, crying out, "Abba, Father!" Therefore you are no longer a slave but a son, and if a son, then an heir of God through Christ (Galatians 4:1-7).*

We are no longer slaves, but sons and daughters! Our context for life has moved from our needing guardians and stewards (external controls) to our being powerful, free children of the living God (see Gal. 3:25-26). Far more is required of those operating in the freedom enjoyed by powerful, rich people than is asked of those living in the limitations endured by slaves. As slaves, we followed the path of least resistance; we weren't required to take full responsibility for our thinking and behavior. We never developed the moral muscles to handle unlimited options. But in the "real world" of the Kingdom, sons and daughters of God are expected to be free; they understand why they are free; and they exercise their freedom toward its purpose—love.

REFLECT

Have you ever seen or experienced honor and confrontation combined? What did it look like? What was the response of the other person(s) involved?

_____

_____

_____

_____

Are you personally governed by external or internal controls? How does this manifest in your life? How does it influence your treatment of others?

_____

_____

_____

_____

Consider the following illustrations from *The Matrix*.

In his first encounter with Morpheus, Neo is told, "…You are a slave, Neo.…like everyone else, …born into bondage…kept inside a prison that you cannot smell, taste, or touch. A prison for your mind."[1]

Morpheus then offers Neo freedom—the red pill. But when Neo wakes up in the "real world," he finds himself on an operating table with all kinds of things sticking out of him. Morpheus explains that they are rebuilding his muscles, which he has never used before. This is a dramatic but clear picture of what it's like for us, who were born *"in bondage under the elements of the world,"* to enter the life of freedom.

Paul goes on to say:

> *For you, brethren, have been called to liberty; only do not use liberty as an opportunity for the flesh, but through love serve one another....I say then: Walk in the Spirit, and you shall not fulfill the lust of the flesh* (Galatians 5:13,16).

Our success in using our freedom to love comes down to *walking by the Spirit*. For this reason, if we as leaders are going to build people who can handle freedom, then our leadership methods must mature to address the *spirit* of people and not simply their *behavior*.

Paul goes on to say: *"Brethren, if a man is overtaken in any trespass, you who are spiritual, restore such a one in a spirit of gentleness, considering yourself lest you also be tempted"* (Gal. 6:1). Paul explains what to do when we cross paths with those who have fallen into the "hole" of sin. In the previous chapter, he described those who are led by the Spirit and express His character (fruit) in their lives. Here he addresses "you who are spiritual" (those who know and display the love and character of God) and declares that we are to handle such situations in "a spirit of gentleness"—one of the fruits of the Spirit.

We are also to be very mindful of the cost of judging others. As Jesus taught, the same judgment that we issue on somebody else's sin will be measured and used against us (see Matt. 7:1-2). The judging of another paints a big target on "the judge" and affords the enemy a turn at us.

REFLECT

What does it look like to address the spirit of a person rather than the behavior?

_____

_____

_____

_____

Have you been prone to focusing on behavior rather than spirit? Why? What objections do you have toward the latter approach? In what ways does it violate your sense of justice?

_____

_____

_____

Gentleness is the perfect term to describe the attitude we must have toward those who have made mistakes or somehow failed. *Gentleness* does not mean "nice," and it doesn't mean "polite." The heart of gentleness is the belief that "I do not need to control you." Those who know the heart of God must carry the reality that they will not attempt to control those who are in trouble. This is the first and most important skill to develop. It is also the most difficult.

Mastery of gentleness begins in our belief system. Do we believe that we can control others? Let's review the simple way to test it out. What happens to you when people do not allow you to control them? Do you become angry? Do you interpret it as "dishonor?" Do you find a way to justify punishing them? A "yes" to any of these questions exposes a lingering belief in the lie that you can and should control people. Kingdom confrontation requires that you repent of this mindset and instead allow others to control themselves.

REFLECT

According to the "tests" described, do you still believe that you can or should control other people? How do you feel about this evaluation of yourself?

_____

_____

_____

_____

What can you do to more fully incorporate gentleness into your belief system and actions?

_____

_____

_____

I had a secret expectation that revival would eliminate all the problems in my environment, and eventually this mindset sneaked up on me. One day I felt a wave of unbelief come over me because of the people problems surrounding me—adultery, child abuse, addictions, lying, and more. I thought to myself, *If God is really here and His Kingdom is coming, then why are so many people still messing up their lives?*

The question caused me to think about the Kingdom of God like I never had before. Is Heaven a place where God controls all the choices? What about The Garden? That place had choices. I realized then that there are poor choices available in Heaven. There have to be poor choices in Heaven, because it's a free place, and Lucifer found a poor choice there. The fact is that when we live in an environment of love and acceptance and apply God's unconditional love to others 100 percent of the time, the sin that lies dormant in their lives (or the sin they have been hiding or struggling with), will come out and end up on the floor.

> "Grace in a culture gives the sin that resides in people's hearts an opportunity to manifest."
> —BILL JOHNSON

We can learn a lesson about the culture of grace by looking at the evolution of pig farming. Pigs are famous for their mess and stench. For centuries, pig farms were the most disgusting environments imaginable. Because pigs have no natural way to cool themselves, farmers provided mudholes for them. The pigs wallowed in the mudholes to keep from overheating. However, the holes would eventually become full of urine and feces. Thus, a powerful stench would permeate the area. Filth, disease, bacteria, and infection were plentiful. But in recent times, someone decided to separate pigs from their mess. Many of today's farmers build facilities designed to protect the pigs from all that is disgusting. Instead of using mud to cool the animals, they use water. The floors and living areas of the pigs have drains and rinse systems that carry the waste away. Pigs can now live in clean environments and be every bit as sanitary as household pets.

The Father paid the highest price of all to make available a new system for dealing with our messes. If humans can figure out how to raise clean pigs and are willing to pay the price for animal cleanliness, the desire of the Father's heart for us will certainly be accomplished by the dear price of Jesus' blood.

Jesus declared, *"You are…clean because of the word which I have spoken to you"* (John 15:3). We are clean!

REFLECT

What do you think of the idea that poor choices are available in Heaven? Have you always assumed that, in a perfect world, God controlled everyone's choices? In what ways does this idea alter your thinking about "ideal" circumstances?

_____

_____

_____

How do you feel about the idea that grace allows people's issues to rise to the surface? Does that seem like a good thing or a bad thing? Why?

_____

_____

_____

_____

Do you truly believe that you are clean, not because of your performance, but because of Christ's performance? Why or why not? How does this affect your view of others?

_____

_____

_____

_____

We need to have a mechanism in our Christian culture that deals effectively with sin when it surfaces right in front of us. For whatever reason, we've come to expect that church is a place where there isn't going to be any sin. It is just not true. If we don't know how to deal with sin, then we don't know how to deal with people. We inevitably create a culture of law in order to keep people from sinning. The message of this culture is, "Contain your sin within yourself. Don't show it to me; I can't handle it."

This was the Pharisees' line. They were famous for being afraid of sin, largely due to the fact that the only remedy for sin in their day was punishment in varying degrees. The fear of punishment ruled their hearts, relationships, and culture. Jesus, on the other hand, had a group of unlikely companions. They were the thieves, tax collectors, and hookers of the day. He was not the least bit afraid of the messes people made or of letting their messes happen around Him. Even the people who'd spent three years walking in personal relationship with Jesus still managed to make messes on the night of His crucifixion. But ultimately, His love and the way He led people empowered them to rise above their mistakes and issues.

REFLECT

Do you feel like you can't handle other people's sins? Do you feel like you don't know what to do with their sins, therefore you'd rather not see them at all? Why or why not?

_____

_____

_____

_____

If we are going to foster a grace culture, we need effective ways of dealing with other people's problems. We need environments that move the waste away from people instead of making it part of who they are. Our methods must accomplish this aim without reinforcing the expectation that we control others and are controlled by them. We have our hands full trying to control ourselves, and no one can control us.

We also need empowering ways of managing *ourselves* in the presence of other people's problems. Our power and peace are rooted in our being able, through self-control, to maintain our freedom around each other. Without the priority of self-control, we live in continual reaction to one another, which creates a culture of blame and irresponsibility. "Your stuff triggers my stuff, and I don't know what to do when you do that. Stop it! Now I am going to blame you for what I do. If you don't do that, I won't have to do this."

People get their power back most quickly in a culture supplied with powerful leaders who lead in freedom and honor. Such a culture recognizes a high value for confrontation, a value that derives from understanding that when messes are not cleaned up, the environment becomes toxic for everyone. However, I want to describe what confrontation is and what it isn't, because there is confusion on that point. The confusion has created plenty of messes *in addition to* the ones the confrontation was meant to address.

REFLECT

Generally speaking, how well do you maintain your self-control? Do you find yourself often blaming other people for your circumstances or reactions, or do you take responsibility for your choices? What can you do to improve in this area?

_____

_____

_____

_____

GOALS OF CONFRONTATION

First, let's identify the goals of confrontation that must be in your heart and must be your motivation as you enter into confrontation. Confrontation is about bringing something to the light. When I come to you in a *spirit of gentleness*, I have come to turn the lights on so that you have an opportunity to *see*. *Gentleness* means that *I do not need to control you*. This confrontation is not an attempt to force your hand or make you do something. It is a loving effort to show you, face to face, what you might not see or know about what you are doing or how you are affecting the world around you. Gentleness is going to help the anxiety remain low and the love increase throughout the process.

Traditionally, confrontation and conflict have been synonymous. These words trigger thoughts of struggle and injury. Too often, the injured parties are people who care about each other. Invariably, the culprit in these struggles is control. The wrong goals produce undesired outcomes. Therefore, it is important to identify and understand the correct goals of confrontation, listed below:

- To introduce consequences into a situation in order to teach and strengthen

- To bring to the surface what people forget about themselves after they have failed

- To send an invitation to strengthen a relational bond with someone

- To apply pressure strategically in order to expose areas needing strength and grace

REFLECT

What is your initial response to these goals? Are there parts you are unsure about or that you believe have been left out? Which of these seems most difficult to you?

_____

_____

_____

_____

Let me explain how *to introduce consequences in order to teach and strengthen.* First, this goal cannot be met until I have dealt with my belief that I can control others. I must have no intention to "get" this person to do something. Instead, this process is designed to help the person see the mess he or she has made and see a helpful ally at his or her side.

Second, I must understand that there is a difference between a *consequence* and a *punishment;* I must be careful to present the former. Many of us are confused on this point because we have heard punishment called *discipline.* We all know that discipline is a good thing—the Bible clearly points out that love and discipline are connected (see Heb. 12:6). Unfortunately, our so-called discipline looks and feels like punishment. It helps us to mask our fear and justify our need for control. There is no power given to the one receiving such "discipline." The one administering it requires complete compliance from the one being "disciplined." Therein is the difference between discipline that amounts to punishment and discipline affected through consequences. Consequences differ from punishment; when consequences are in play, power is given to the one who has made the mess.

REFLECT

Have you generally worked with consequences or punishment? What has been the result in your relationships?

_____

_____

_____

_____

How do consequences give power to the one who has made the mess?

_____

_____

_____

_____

The process of Kingdom confrontation is a process of empowerment, not domination. When a person fails and generates a consequence for the failure, the confrontation leads and empowers the person to clean up the mess. One of our sayings at Bethel is: "Feel free to make as big a mess as you are ready to clean up." This is not a flippant broadcast of irresponsibility. It is simply a message to everyone that personal responsibility is required in this environment. No one will be stuck with your mess, and no one can clean up the mess you made as well as you can.

At Bethel, our interventions are built upon the expectation that people motivated by respect for relationships will respond by taking ownership for their choices and the consequences that come from them. This response is only possible when people know they are free. They are free to blow the whole thing off. Only then can they choose to clean up their messes. Only then can they choose to honor and respect their community and relationships. If we steal this option from them because we want to control the outcome, then we disempower them and create powerless, irresponsible victims. Powerless victims never own anything; nor do they change their circumstances. Therefore, our confrontations must carry the goal of empowerment from the start. Our process of confrontation will point to the consequences of their choices and offer strength and wisdom instead of control and punishment.

REFLECT

How do you feel about the statement, "Feel free to make as big a mess as you are ready to clean up"? What attitude does it convey?

_____

_____

_____

_____

Do you want people to have the option of "blowing the whole thing off"? Why or why not? What does this reveal about your beliefs in regard to controlling others?

_____

_____

_____

_____

Why doesn't powerlessness result in people changing their circumstances and choices? Why does feeling powerful have the opposite effect? When have you felt powerless? When have you felt powerful? What difference can you see in your responses in these situations?

_____

_____

_____

The next goal of confrontation is *to bring to the surface what people forget about themselves after they have failed*. In a culture of rules, not only do people expect punishment for their failures, but they are also overwhelmed by the power of shame. According to the size of their mistakes or their sensitivity to failure, shame takes root in their hearts. Shame isn't just a feeling; it is a *spirit* that attacks the identities of individuals. This spirit lies to people and leads them to believe that their poor behavior is really flowing from who they are: "You didn't fail; you are a failure!"

The greatness that resides at the core of every believer must come forth if we are to truly represent our Father in Heaven. Putting on the cloak of shame and guilt is not only unbecoming for us as His sons and daughters, but it is also a trap of powerlessness. Reaching in and grabbing our people by their true identities is an act of love that will live on far longer than the sting of failure and consequences. People can see and think when their identities are clear of fear and shame. Again and again, we have seen the greatness in people who have made mistakes, but then took charge and worked evil into good. And right along with this, we see our covenant relationships strengthened and deepened.

REFLECT

Have you ever had someone do this for you—remind you of your true identity in the midst of your failure? What impact did this have on you?

_____

_____

_____

_____

Our next goal in confrontation is to extend *an invitation to strengthen a relational bond with someone*. We must see the process of bringing an issue to the light as an invitation to practice our covenant relationships. It may appear that our priority is to settle a matter or change a behavior. In reality, Kingdom confrontation is a test of the covenant between two or more people; the relationship is always the true priority.

When you hold another person accountable for his or her impact on you or the surrounding community, you expose the levels of trust the two of you share. When, through confrontation, you test the connection that binds you, you will learn the true strength of the covenant you have with that person.

Trust is the key to a successful confrontation. Without it, you will discover your limitations quickly. If and when you find a confrontation going poorly, the first thing to check is the trust level. When trust is low, anxiety is usually high. When anxiety rises, the priority in the encounter shifts to self-preservation, usually by means of control-seeking. If you are face to face with a person who feels compelled to self-protect, then you are not talking to the person's greatness, but to his or her survival tactics. To have trust, the person you confront must believe that you are an ally who will protect his or her best interests throughout the confrontation.

REFLECT

In confrontation, is your focus more often on the issue at hand or on the relational connection? Why? In what ways has this helped or hindered your success in confrontation?

Why does a lack of trust result in an increase in anxiety? How have you seen this play out in your own life? What practical things can you do to build trust in the midst of a confrontation?

Our final goal is to *apply pressure strategically in order to expose areas needing strength and grace.* We need to find the "broken spots" and begin healing them. My best analogy for "applying pressure" comes from my early adult years working in a tire store. One of my duties was to repair logging-truck tires. After removing the inner tube, I would connect the air hose to the stem of the inner tube and fill it with far more air than the tube could contain while inside the tire. Once the tube was stretched to capacity, I would take it over to a tank filled with water and systematically submerge portions of the tube. As I held the tube under the water, I would roll the tube under my hands and hunt for bubbles. I was trying to find the "broken spot" by spotting where the air was leaking out. As soon as I figured out where the bubbles were coming from, I would mark the tube and repair it. The point is that the process only worked when I filled the inner tube with enough internal pressure to expose the "broken spot." The break in the tube never revealed itself until the right amount of pressure was applied.

External pressure will never expose someone's "broken spot." Yelling at it, threatening to cut it into little pieces, coaxing it, or interrogating it are never going to help expose the spot that needs healing. This work is accomplished from the inside out. Confrontation is a process of applying pressure to another person's life—on purpose—to expose the broken spots. We need to find these places if we ever hope to arrest the destructive loops in which so many people live. Simply put, they cannot make different decisions and create different results until they know what is wrong.

Isaiah 1:18 says: "'Come now, and let us reason together,' says the Lord, 'Though your sins are like scarlet....'" In other words, though your sins are blatantly exposed, God says, "We can do something about that." There is hope. The very heartbeat, nature, and desire of God is for us to come to Him. In the words, "reason together," the Lord invites us to mutually examine the issue in order to correct it. God does not need to control us, and is He not afraid of our "broken spots." He knows that we can truly change only when we are free to change.

REFLECT

Why is internal pressure so much more effective than external pressure? What has your experience been in confrontation? Have people primarily used internal or external pressure on you? How did it feel? What sort of pressure have you used with others?

_____

_____

_____

_____

CREATING INTERNAL PRESSURE

The power of confrontation comes from the inside out. It has to be genuinely motivated from the inside if it has a prayer of lasting. A common mistake we make is leading someone to say something seemingly magical like "I'm sorry." But the solutions to relational disconnection and injury come from the heart, not through simple formulas. Getting at the heart requires a process that creates internal pressure.

Over and over we see Jesus demonstrate this process. He asked a man who was obviously blind, *"What do you want Me to do for you?"* This man's first name was "Blind," as in Blind Bartimaeus! Of course, the man answered, *"I want to regain my sight!"* (Mark 10:51 NASB). Why did the Lord ask such an obvious question? Or why, when He approached the lame man at the Pool of Bethesda—a man who had been waiting there for 18 years hoping to catch the angel stirring the water—did He ask, *"Do you wish to get well?"* (John 5:6 NASB). Why did the Man whose healing ministry had a 100 percent success rate stop and ask questions with seemingly obvious answers? Herein lies the power of internal pressure.

Jesus understood and practiced the truth that people are born to be free. If we do not have the power to choose, we will never be responsible for the choice. In God's presence is freedom: freedom to think, decide, and own our lives. Jesus asked the blind and lame these questions because there is a line of demarcation between where one life stops and another life starts. If we believe that we can control others or that we should control others in order to demonstrate our great love, then there is no line. We operate on a faulty premise that says, "Your life belongs to me when I want something *from* you or *for* you."

If we do not have the power to choose, we will never be responsible for the choice.

But, if I am to honor your life and your self-control, then there must be a line where I stop and you start—and both of us must honor that line. Creating internal pressure is an appropriate way to honor the line. Great questions serve a number of benefits in a successful confrontation:

- They stimulate thinking within the individual whose problem is at issue.

- They allow the person doing the thinking to solve the problem from the inside out.

- They help the person tap into and display his or her greatness during the confrontation.

- They remind the person of things they tend to forget about themselves in failure.

- They demonstrate the covenant relationship between the two parties.

- They allow the one doing the confronting to remain an ally.

REFLECT

What do you think of the idea of creating internal pressure? Does it seem too difficult, or are you beginning to understand how it works?

_____

_____

_____

_____

How do questions maintain the boundaries between individuals? Why is this important in confrontation? Why is controlling someone into doing the "right thing" not an act of love?

_____

_____

_____

_____

WHO IS "CONFRONTABLE?"

In Genesis 18 there is a great story about two friends—Abraham and God. It is an absolutely amazing example to me that God is a real person. He is not some cosmic perfection that has zero need or tolerance for me. Nor is He the "Big Boss upstairs" who insists He either gets His way or somebody's got to die. Watch this:

> *Then the men rose from there and looked toward Sodom, and Abraham went with them to send them on the way. And the Lord said, "Shall I hide from Abraham what I am doing, since Abraham shall surely become a great and mighty nation, and all the nations of the earth shall be blessed in him?"* (Genesis 18:16-18)

God was on His way to destroy Sodom. But, first He was going to check in with His friend Abraham, who might have something to say about it. God told him that the outcry against Sodom was great and that He must do something about it. Abraham's response? *"And Abraham came near and said, 'Would You also destroy the righteous with the wicked?'"* (Gen. 18:23).

Then came the questions:

Suppose there were fifty righteous within the city; would You also destroy the place and not spare it for the fifty righteous that were in it? Far be it from You to do such a thing as this, to slay the righteous with the wicked, so that the righteous should be as the wicked; far be it from You! Shall not the Judge of all the earth do right? (Genesis 18:24-25)

While being confronted by Abraham, God stood there and responded, "Yeah, you are right. I would spare the city for fifty righteous men." This is profound! God is confrontable! It is unusual, because we've come to know leadership as being unconfrontable.

We classically interpret the confrontation of leadership as a form of dishonor. God and Abraham did not see it this way. At God's response, Abraham continued to progressively whittle down the size of the group to ensure God's mercy on the city: "OK," said Abraham, "forty… thirty…twenty…ten—how many are too few for You to care, God?"

Abraham threw in a couple of questions, and made it clear that he did not mean any disrespect along the way. In the end *"…the Lord went His way as soon as He finished speaking with Abraham; and Abraham returned to his place"* (Gen. 18:33).

Abraham trusted God, and God trusted Abraham. If God made Himself open to confrontation by a man, it begs the question: who is above confrontation? A safe environment is filled with powerful, free people; if it isn't, it will quickly become an unsafe place controlled by those who think they have all the power.

REFLECT

What do you think of the idea that even God is confrontable? What can you learn from Abraham's example of confrontation in this passage?

_____

_____

_____

_____

Have you generally believed that confronting leaders is dishonoring? Why or why not? What is the proper way to confront a leader?

_____

_____

_____

THE KEY INGREDIENT IS TRUST

If you know that I value you greatly, then you will feel free to invite my input. If you trust that I have your best interest at heart, we can engage in confrontation to build a deeper covenant relationship. If you get a whiff that I don't respect or value you, you will protect yourself from my help. This is the classic problem of adolescent/parent dynamics: the child becomes a young man or young woman and feels the parent's disrespect for his or her ability to think and make decisions. The adolescent doesn't feel trusted and, therefore, resists confrontation.

The nature of godly confrontation is truth. The purpose of creating internal pressure is to find the truth, not to get a confession. People who cannot trust will not disclose the truth of what is going on inside them to anyone. They feel safer keeping the "broken spot" concealed. It takes a safe place to expose a vulnerable area that needs healing. For this reason, the confronter's belief that he or she holds great authority and should be trusted, matters far less than the scared person's belief that he or she is being cared for and protected.

REFLECT

Do you like sharing your heart with or receiving correction from people who don't respect you or value your decision-making abilities? Why or why not? How does this revelation affect your confrontations with others? Are you prone to looking down on those you need to confront, or do you honor them as competent people who can fix their own problems?

_____

_____

_____

_____

In essence, a confrontation is an examination. It is a procedure that trusts another to look at some part of your life that you may not know about or understand. It is both a vulnerable and necessary process if we expect to build healthy lives and live in peace. King David put it this way:

Search me, O God, and know my heart; try me, and know my anxieties; and see if there is any wicked way in me, and lead me in the way everlasting (Psalm 139:23-24).

Jesus is the Great Confronter. One of the keys to His mastery of confrontation is that His interactions with people were motivated by compassion. He was neither afraid in the presence of their mistakes nor afraid to confront them with a loving invasion of the truth. Whether with His disciples, the rich young ruler, or the woman at the well, He was better able than anyone to help people identify what was going on below the surface. Children, who are naturals at identifying safety, recognized Jesus as a safe place. They instinctively trusted Him and ran up to Him with abandon.

> "If it doesn't hurt you to confront another person, you probably have a wrong attitude."
> —BILL JOHNSON

Confrontation and empowerment go hand in hand in a culture of honor; mercy, compassion, and courage are the qualities necessary for maintaining a healthy flow of these two elements in your environment. Successful confrontation builds relationships and strengthens covenant bonds. It is an art built on certain skills, but more importantly, it is a lifestyle that flows from your beliefs and core values. The more you establish Heaven's goals for confrontation in your thinking, the more you will be positioned to release Heaven into your relationships.

REFLECT

What about confrontation do you find scary? Why? How do you usually respond to confrontation? What value do you see confrontation having in your own life?

_____

_____

_____

_____

Do you usually confront people with compassion? What does this look like? What can you do to increase your level of compassion and your empowerment of others in confrontation?

_____

_____

_____

_____

TOOL: AVOIDING ABUSIVE HONOR

1. Understand the target of honor: For some reason, people want *honor* to be something that other people give to them. From the beginning, regardless of the circumstances, *honor is what we give to others.* Honor is nothing less than two people working together to meet the needs of one another and the needs of the situation.

2. Understand the quest of honor:

   - Determine to develop the skills and conviction to give honor to others regardless of their political, spiritual, or core values.

   - Decide to meet the needs of others in their relationship with you. In order to have honoring relationships, this must be a primary motivator. Honestly examine your beliefs about this, and identify any ways in which you have expected others to *first* be willing to meet your needs. Proactively address these areas by choosing to prioritize the needs of others.

   - Learn to build relationships with people who are very different from you. Honestly examine your life to see whether honor has been your driving force, or whether you have been driven by agreement instead. When encountering people who are different from you, consciously remind yourself of the values of honor, and mentally release these people to believe differently. Choose not to be afraid of your differences.

DISCUSS

Discuss these questions with a friend or in a small group:

1. It goes against most people's gut reactions to respond to a person's spirit rather than behavior. Why is this? Why is it important to focus on the spirit rather than the behavior? What changes can you make to help you refocus in the midst of confrontation?

2. Discuss the idea that Heaven has poor choices in it. How do you feel about this? What does it tell you about God? In what ways does it change the way you think about sin?

3. Why is trust so important in confrontation? Share a time when you felt trust in a confrontation and a time when you didn't. Compare the results of each example. What practical steps can you take to communicate that you are "a safe

place" (one who can be trusted) so that others will not fear opening themselves to your examination?

APPLY

1. Think of a recent confrontation that you initiated. According to the standards of confrontation in this chapter, evaluate how well you honored and empowered the person you were confronting. If you did not do well, ask yourself what you were afraid of in the situation. Were you trying to control the other person? Replay the scene in your mind and rewrite the "script" from a place of love rather than fear.

2. From the list of goals for great questions on page #, make a list of questions that would serve these goals in future confrontations. Practice using them in life's small everyday confrontations, so that they replace fear as your natural response.

3. When faced with someone else's sin (especially sin that hurts or disappoints you), how likely are you to try to control that person and the circumstances? What heart issues are causing this impulse to control? Ask God to reveal to you the lies you have believed and to heal the areas of brokenness that He reveals. Regularly remind yourself: "I'm successful today if I am able to simply control *myself*."

ENDNOTE

1. Larry Wachowski and Andy Wachowski, *The Matrix*, script posted by IMSDb, http://www.imsdb.com/scripts/Matrix,-The.html (accessed January 13, 2011).

Chapter 8

REVOLUTION TO REFORMATION TO TRANSFORMATION

There was a time in our nation's history when it was considered acceptable to own human beings. We passed down a cultural view and practice that slavery was "necessary" in order for commerce and our households to function. We enslaved, sold, oppressed, and punished people like animals because it was "normal" to do so. The most difficult aspect of this tragedy is that it was seemingly biblical. Both the Old and New Testaments apparently condone and show God's blessing on slave owners. The apostle Paul instructed slaves to submit to their masters (see Eph. 6:5; Col. 3:22). Jesus did not instruct His disciples to "set My people free" and wage a campaign against slavery.

Or did He? Jesus introduced His ministry by stating that He had been anointed *"to proclaim liberty to the captives"* (Luke 4:18). He later commissioned all who would follow Him to imitate His example. This leaves each generation of believers to answer the question of how to do that. How can we violate our own Scriptures, and especially our traditions, to find a higher place of honor and freedom for people?

It usually takes a war. As the history of our nation proves, it sometimes takes a civil war.

Uncle Tom's Cabin, written by Harriet Beecher Stowe, is considered by many historians to have significantly influenced events leading to the Civil War, which ended in the abolition of slavery in America. But Stowe's brother and fellow abolitionist, Henry Ward Beecher, gave another man credit for the overthrow of slavery, saying, "Rev. John Rankin and his sons did it."[1]

In her book, *Beyond the River: The Untold Stories of the Heroes of the Underground Railroad*, Ann Hagedorn describes the life and work of John Rankin, who was born in Tennessee and raised in a strict Calvinist home. In 1800, Rankin's eighth year of life, his view of the world and his religious faith were deeply affected by two things: the revivals of the Second Great Awakening[2] that were sweeping through the Appalachian region and the largest organized (though unsuccessful) slave rebellion in U.S. history up to that point, led by an enslaved man, Gabriel Prosser, who was executed along with 27 of his conspirators. Hagedorn writes:

> For Rankin, the events of his eighth year resonated deeply. In his memory, the story of a man losing his life in pursuit of freedom would always blend together with the many nights of manifestation in the woodlands of East Tennessee. There would come a time when enough years had passed that Rankin could look back and know that the passions of the summer of 1800 had inspired his own private awakening.[3]

Convinced that the thrust of the Gospel was to eradicate from the world oppression in general and slavery in particular, Rankin wrestled deeply with the portions of Scripture that seemed to condone slavery. Ultimately he resolved this conflict by determining that the balance of the Word taught that God never intended humankind to be enslaved and that it was the duty of every righteous man and woman to seek God's highest purposes for humankind.

The passion birthed in Rankin's heart as a young boy ultimately led him to brave dangers of all kinds from angry, rotten-egg-slinging[4] mobs to slanderous newspapers and direct physical attacks on him, his family, and his property. He was not only fearless and unstoppable in preaching the message of freedom, but also in living it. He and his family continually spent their time and resources to help runaway slaves reach freedom; they also supported other abolitionists in their efforts to do the same.

Henry Ward Beecher, who observed Rankin's heroism firsthand, believed this one man's message and example were so powerful that the dismantling of an entire system of oppression (a system that many, even those who decried it, believed impossible to remove) has been laid to his credit.

REFLECT

What most impacts you about Rankin's story? Have you ever experienced anything similar to the resolve that Rankin found through the events of his eighth year? Explain.

The life of John Rankin is evidence that when Heaven touches Earth in revival, it creates two things inside us—a vision of what God created the world to be and a cry to take part in the restoration of all things until it is truly *"on earth as it is in heaven"* (Matt. 6:10). Encountering the living God and receiving a fresh revelation of His heart give us a greater hunger for freedom in our own lives and require us to "set the captives free" (see Luke 4:18). This appetite drives us past the cultural norms and fuels us with supernatural courage to spurn the persecution that comes from those maintaining the status quo. Revival ignites in people the life needed to press against the limitations and boundaries of society. It calls to the deepest parts of humankind and screams, "Freedom!" so loudly that the same cry comes out of our mouths. *Revival* launches *revolution* and revolution initiates *reformation*.

This is where we stand as a movement in our generation. We are in the throes of a reformation. No longer will we tolerate the status quo of an externally-governed existence. No longer will we accept training in powerlessness. No longer will we live as servants and slaves. The religious motivation of the pending wrath of God and the ideals of a small life are no longer options for us. We are sons and daughters of the Most High. We are in training for reigning as never before. We now expect to be powerful and to live abundant lives in Christ until the kingdoms of this earth become the Kingdom of our God.

REFLECT

Have you experienced revival in your personal life, as described here? Does the proclamation of freedom in these paragraphs resonate within you? What fire has revival ignited within you?

How does a passion for freedom in people's lives relate to the subject of honor? How can you personally connect the two in your life?

I have the privilege of leading the Bethel School of Transformation. This four-day school provides people with a behind-the-scenes peek at the culture of freedom we are building at Bethel. Without exception, there has been a senior leader in every school who asks, "How in the world are we ever going to do this in our church?"

You are not alone if you have that question. Let me share a testimony about a good friend of mine who had this same question. Steve Doerter, a pastor in North Carolina, got involved in the Bethel culture a couple of years ago. He began to listen to the podcasts, came to some conferences, and began to bring the things he was learning to his congregation and its other leaders. These things represented some significant changes for these people. The church historically was Baptist, had become non-denominational, and under Steve's leadership pursued more freedom and power than they ever had before. However, they had not yet come to know what he experienced at Bethel, and they found it difficult to be on the same page with him.

REFLECT

Have you struggled with this same question? In what ways do you find it difficult to take the ideas you are learning and transmit them into your environment and the lives of people around you?

_____

_____

_____

_____

Eventually Steve decided to expose his leaders to what he was pursuing by bringing them to Bethel's Leader's Advance conference, an invitation-only conference for leaders who are in relationship with other leaders in our network. One night at the Advance, my wife Sheri and I sat at dinner with Steve, his wife, Joyce, and his leadership board. They were a friendly enough group, but they obviously did not understand much of what was going on around them. At the Leader's Advance, our School of Supernatural Ministry students wait on the tables. These students are constantly "under the influence" of the Holy Spirit, and on this particular night, our table waiters became increasingly drunk. They were happy—super happy. Finally, Steve's leaders asked, "What is wrong with those people?"

I replied, "They're just happy, and they're drunk."

"They're drunk?" they asked.

I explained, "There is a guy named Georgian Banov. He is upstairs in another dining room praying for people, and I would imagine that the whole upstairs is drunk by now. You should go up there and check it out! You should just go look at it—get close enough to see it."

They said, "Well, we'd like to do that. We'd like to go see what this is." And off they went.

REFLECT

What was happening with the students who were "drunk"? How is this part of a culture of honor and freedom? What aspects of it, if any, cause you to feel anxious or concerned?

_____

_____

_____

_____

The next report I got was that they eventually had their own pile—that is, their own pile of former Baptist elders. The next time I saw these distinguished people, their hair was all messed up and one had his pant leg tucked into his shoe. It was then that I could see Steve gaining momentum with his leadership team.

Since Steve's team attended that conference, there have been several significant miracles in their church. Cancerous tumors have disappeared in a woman's body. Financial miracles, inner healings, and deliverances are now a common part of this church's day-to-day experience. A three-year-old boy named Pablo, who was diagnosed with a developmental disorder that falls within the spectrum of autism, was healed after Pastor Steve preached a sermon entitled, "God is Good, and I Highly Recommend Him." He talked about the goodness of God, the faithfulness of God, and God's heart toward people. He shared testimonies and stirred faith in the room.

At the end of the message, Pablo's mom came up for prayer, and several leaders laid hands on her, in proxy for him. They began to command healing, the release of miracles, and the release of Heaven into their situation at home. Since then, Pablo's improvement has been incredible. Even the principal of Pablo's school has testified, "This is nothing short of a miracle that has happened in our city."

REFLECT

What connection do you see between what happened with the church's leadership team and the ensuing outbreak of miracles at their church?

_____

_____

_____

_____

Write in your own words a brief explanation of the connection between the culture of honor and the supernatural. How has this played a part in your life? What can you do to increase it?

_____

_____

_____

_____

- Revolution: A forcible overthrow of a government or social order in favor of a new system

- Reformation: The action or process of reforming an institution or practice

- Transformation: A thorough or dynamic change in form or appearance

REVOLUTIONARIES

A revolution is happening, and you are a witness to it. In fact, if you have made it this far in this book, then you are most likely a participant in it. You are a revolutionary! Your involvement as a revolutionary is going to lead us to our next great reformation in the Church. We are in the midst of a great transformation. Heaven is infiltrating the Body of Christ and stirring up the passion and the hearts of those who have come to expect more.

Momentum is developing, and more and more people are hearing about the "leaking through" of Heaven to Earth. Everywhere members of our team go to minister, people tell us, "Heaven is leaking through, and our city is starting to hear about it." There is something happening all around the globe. We are starting to feel part of a momentum…part of a movement…part of a transformation.

Revolution is defined as "A forcible overthrow of a government or social order in favor of a new system." This definition is begging to be associated with Matthew 11:12: *"…the kingdom of heaven suffers violence, and violent men take it by force"* (NASB). As the Kingdom advances in revival, it is bringing about a forcible overthrow of Church government, the forcible challenge of a social order to which so many of us have been confined throughout our Church experience. There is a way of doing things that has constrained Heaven from blasting the earth. But someone somewhere has said, "Enough! I've had enough of this!" And it has begun a revolution.

REFLECT

How do you feel about the idea that the government of the Church is being overthrown? In what ways have you or haven't you participated in this revolution? What affect has it had upon you?

_____

_____

_____

_____

We have begun a revolution that is leading to a reformation, and a *reformation* is simply this: "the action or process of reforming an institution or practice." Institutions develop because the way of doing things becomes so comfortable, predictable, and routine, that we no longer have to think, risk, or believe. It's all simply a matter of rote behavior; it carries us through our Christian lives because it is the way we've always done it. A reformation is something that comes and forces a pointed question: "Everything you've known has changed. Now, what are you going to do?"

The answer is that we're going to have to create something we've never seen before.

REFLECT

Write down your answer to the question, "Everything you've known has changed. Now, what are you going to do?" How has the material in this book helped you form your answer?

_____

_____

When reformation is complete, it brings transformation: "A thorough or dramatic change in form or appearance." Our transformation demonstrates to the world that it's something brand-new, something that no one has ever seen before. We are living in a time, in a day, and in a government that allows us to change. We now are living in a posture and in a relationship with our city that looks completely different from that of the past. However, I need to be honest about one necessary element in this transformation that can be a deal-breaker for a lot of people: It's common for people to say, "We want to change. We want things to be different. We went to a conference and things are going to be different now. We bought the whole video set, and now, buddy, things are going be different around here." Except there's this one piece that they miss: they have a whole herd of sacred cows that do not want to budge.

REFLECT

What transformation—what brand-new thing—is evident in your life? What impact is this having on the people and environment around you?

_____

_____

_____

_____

What "sacred cows" might you be holding on to? In what areas do you find yourself resistant to change? Why?

_____

_____

_____

_____

Recently, I found a brochure stuck in the screen door at our house. It was from a church in our neighborhood. Across the top, it read: "Not Like Every Other Church." I opened the brochure because I hoped it was true. On the front was a picture of the pastor and his wife and their names. We'll call them Mr. and Mrs. Ed Jones. Below were pictures of several other couples. We'll call them, Mr. and Mrs. Tom Smith, Mr. and Mrs. Ozzie Wald, Mr. and Mrs. Harry Chin, and so on.

As I read the brochure, I thought, *There are two people in each of these pictures, but only one first name is listed in each case. Who is the woman in each photo? Where did she go? This isn't any different. This is the same old malarkey. The closer a woman gets to that church, the more she disappears. That is a scary place if you're a woman.*

The Church is one of the last institutions in our society that practices sexism freely and "biblically." For some reason, the dishonoring and disempowerment of our women is still tolerated. The brochure was a lie; that church wasn't unlike most churches. It isn't hard to say that everything's different, but too often everything still looks and feels virtually the same, with the same anxiety and control still in place. Revolutionaries know that transformation comes when we are finally willing to have a "sacred-cow barbecue."

REFLECT

What do you think of this example about women in the church? In what ways does it make you feel anxious or uncomfortable? What do you need to do in your own life to eliminate dishonor toward women? If you are a woman, how do you need to change your self-perception to more fully honor and value your womanhood?

_____

_____

_____

_____

What sacred cows in your own life and church is God asking you to barbecue?

_____

_____

_____

_____

GOVERNMENTAL SHIFTS

In Chapters 2 and 3, I explained the governmental shifts that are necessary for Heaven to flow to the earth. Transformation has been successful at Bethel to the degree that we have implemented a new set of core values and paradigms. The government that is typically in place in our churches (and has been for centuries) is what I refer to as a pastoral government, with a pastoral directive. It features the following players at the helm: pastors, administrators, teachers, and even evangelists. Once again, the priorities of this government are where the problems start. The following chart describes the priorities in each case:

CURRENT GOVERNMENT	CURRENT PRIORITIES
Pastors	People
Administrators	Things
Teachers	Doctrine
Evangelists	Salvation Message

The first priority in a pastoral government is *people*. How safe, comfortable, and happy are the people in our church environment? We can pretend like we don't, but this governing system cares about "butts in the seat." The next priority is our *things*. In a pastoral government, there are many teachings about stewardship and taking care of our money, our parking lot, our building, our stuff. These are the driving forces of how we do church. The next priority, *doctrine*, leads us to focus on right and wrong, truth and error. We end up trying to teach people to defend themselves against other Christians, to defend their lives as believers, and to defend their choice of and participation in a particular church. The *Gospel of salvation* is the final priority. Getting people saved is generally the only supernatural activity in the pastoral environment. And without the presence of the supernatural, we end up teaching converts a conflicted message: "You were a sinner; you prayed a prayer; and now God's grace is applied to your life. But you're still a sinner and we're watching you."

REFLECT

In what ways are these priorities evident in your life and church? Which of these feels very important to you and would be hard for you to relinquish? Why?

The core values of this environment flow from its leadership anointing and structure. For example, here's a core value that has been propagated liberally among the congregations of our nation: "God is always right, so be like Him. Be one of the most difficult people on the planet to talk to. We have taught you the truth, and don't you dare consider anything except what we taught you because you might be deceived. Someone might introduce you to the idea that the supernatural is part of the Kingdom of Heaven. The 'supernatural' is always suspect and full of deceptions. Only the devil has supernatural power on the earth."

Such core values create an environment centered on the things that can be proved and controlled. If you're in a pastoral government, you're going to have some problems trying to introduce contrary core values to that environment. The pastoral priorities are not evil, any more than childhood is evil. They are, however, an inferior representation of Christianity. A system that effectively prevents believers from growing up causes symptoms of disorder. People don't grow as God designed them to in a pastoral environment because, deep in its core, the pastoral government defines its people as sinners working out their salvation. This means that the people are not trustworthy and are essentially servants waiting for further instructions. Our lives are defined by a divine to-do list.

These are some of the sacred cows that need to find their way to the "grill." It's scary to say that doctrine isn't the most important part of our relationship with God. And even to suggest that the salvation message isn't paramount can seem like heresy. But until we are willing to reorder our thinking by being renewed in our minds, then yesterday will determine our tomorrow.

REFLECT

How do you feel about the statement that the priorities of a pastoral government comprise an inferior Christianity?

_____

_____

_____

_____

How could doctrine and the salvation message be sacred cows? If you are willing to accept this statement, what might it mean for your life?

_____

_____

_____

_____

We must have permission in our church environments to challenge the sacred cows of our day, just as Jesus did. One of the primary things we must confront is the issue of order in the house of God. We do that with Scripture:

> *God has appointed in the church, first apostles, second prophets, third teachers, then miracles, then gifts of healings, helps, administrations, various kinds of tongues* (1 Corinthians 12:28 NASB).

When a new young lion takes over the leadership of a pride, the first thing he does is kill all the cubs of the old lion. This action causes all of the females to go into heat so the new leader can breed an entire new bloodline that will carry his DNA. I watched Bill Johnson do that at Bethel Church. When Bill landed at Bethel, it had a pastoral government, led by an evangelist. Through a series of massive shifts, Bill introduced a new government that was aligned with what Paul laid out: *"First apostles, second prophets, third teachers…"* and thereby introduced a new set of priorities:

NEW GOVERNMENT	NEW PRIORITIES
Apostles	Heaven
Prophets	Spirit World
Teachers	Articulation of the Kingdom
Workers of Miracles	Supernatural Activity of the Believers

In this government, the priorities are about Heaven, the presence of God, and the blueprint of Heaven being reproduced on the earth. There are new core values for the activity of the spirit world, for the saints having their eyes and ears opened by the prophet, for hearing the heartbeat of Heaven and becoming aware of the activity of the third Heaven, which supersedes the devil's strategies. Signs, wonders, and miracles bring people into "God encounters" that radically change the way life is lived here on the earth. No longer is it an environment of fear and reaction, but of proactively establishing the architecture and blueprint of Heaven on the earth—of making the prayer *"Your Kingdom come. Your will be done on earth as it is in heaven"* (Matt. 6:10) a reality for believers and the community around them.

REFLECT

What do you think of this new set of priorities as compared to the former set? Which set resonates most in your heart? Why? What aspects make you uncomfortable?

_____

_____

_____

_____

In what ways have you seen these priorities manifesting in your life? Are you and those around you encountering the supernatural regularly? Explain.

_____

_____

_____

_____

Once again, the role of the teacher in this new government changes: no longer does the teacher build a defensive network so the flock can stand against other believers or cults. The teacher's job is to help people see Heaven and a supernatural God at work on the earth via Scripture. They provide a biblical context for understanding the apostles and prophets and their core values. If the people do not understand what is happening in this new paradigm, they will be afraid and seek a place where they can be in charge again. Teachers help bring this understanding and reduce the anxiety of God's people that would otherwise keep them from entering into the fullness of what is available in His presence.

REFLECT

Have you encountered a teacher who has helped explain the supernatural priorities of Heaven for you? In what ways has the presence or absence of a properly-functioning teacher influenced your life?

_____

_____

_____

_____

I want to give attention to the next role Paul mentions in this particular list: the workers of miracles. I believe that "workers of miracles" is another description of the role of the evangelist in an apostolic government. I believe we have lost the connection between these two roles because, without the leadership of apostles and prophets, workers of miracles generally don't get to operate in their roles. But in an apostolic environment, the apostles and prophets pull the supernatural into the environment, and the workers of miracles run around pushing every button to see what can happen. They bring the priority of supernatural activity into the practical, daily lives of believers, as well as to the lives of all those in their community, along with a high value for protecting that activity. They create a contagion for risk-taking and living in the impossible.

As the new wineskin of apostolic leadership is established, a new wave of evangelism is released through the workers of miracles. For the past century, the Church has emphasized the practice of evangelism, which has brought many into the Kingdom. It is also something most modern Christians are trained to do in their local congregations. But the workers of miracles are bringing a new practice of evangelism into the Church's environment. These radicals of faith are releasing "God encounters" everywhere they go. Healings, miracles, words of knowledge, prophetic ministry, and heavenly revelation are leading people to Jesus in droves.

REFLECT

What do you think of this connection between evangelists and workers of miracles? Have you witnessed or participated in supernaturally empowered evangelism? How did it impact you? How did it impact the people who were being reached out to?

_____

_____

_____

_____

Where I come from, we call these workers of miracles "treasure hunters." Teams of people pray together and get a "treasure list" from Heaven. This list has things like names, places, colors of clothing, specific areas of the body that have pain, diseases, situations in people's lives, gender, and all kinds of other "clues." The team then goes out into the community to find their "treasure." As soon as a "treasure hunter" locates someone on the list, he or she approaches and shows the person that he or she is on the "treasure list." At this point, the "treasure hunter" asks if there is something that he or she can pray about for the person. Time after time, Heaven rocks these people. God shows up in power! Signs, wonders, and miracles are the ongoing testimony of "treasure hunting." Although many people give their hearts to Jesus in these encounters, it isn't the primary goal. The priority is for believers to be conduits on the Earth for Heaven to happen. We are creating opportunities for the blueprint of Heaven to be expressed.

REFLECT

Have you ever participated in a "treasure hunt"? What was your experience? What about it is intimidating for you? What about it is most fulfilling and exciting?

_____

_____

_____

_____

TRANSFORMING CITIES WITH HONOR

Another priority of an apostolic mission is to leak the Kingdom into the community rather drawing the community to come to our church. This priority is motivated by honor and a wealth mindset, which lead us to look for ways to benefit those around us.

I want to tell you about a friend of mine who is seeing the blueprint unfold in his Mexican city. His name is Angel Nava. He and his wife, Esther, lead a church and school of supernatural ministry in the southern portion of Baja, California, in a city called La Paz (Peace). When Esther first saw the power of God at work in a meeting with Bill Johnson and Kris Vallotton, she knew she had discovered the reason she was alive. Angel, on the other hand, was scared of the supernatural manifestations and wanted nothing to do with them. But the Lord slowly brought him to a place of curiosity and finally to the place where he recognized that Heaven was trying to invade his city. He and Esther purposed to do whatever they needed to do in order to welcome God into La Paz.

Their first step was to partner with Denny and Danette Taylor, who were sent out from Bethel to bring a school of supernatural ministry into their city. As they did, they immediately began to see healings and miracles. In the first year of the school, they saw a woman raised from the dead. As new and exciting as this was in their lives and ministry, Angel's heart was to see his city transformed. He wanted to better understand what was needed on his end for Heaven to be welcome in Mexico. He began to realize that God was in a good mood and wanted people to know His love. He also started to believe that his great city could experience God more effectively if he helped Jesus get out of the church and into the streets. But how was he to do that? All he had known up to that point was how to go into the city and bring people back to his church. He needed a strategy change.

Mexico does not have a blood-donor system that works. There is a government official responsible to receive blood donations, but no one donates blood. It is customary for Mexican citizens to find their own donors when they need transfusions. Angel got an idea. He went into his local blood donation department and talked to the new director about how his job was going. Aware that business was slow, Angel asked some questions about how blood donation worked in La Paz. The following week, he shared his new city-transformation strategy with his congregation: "We will become the largest donors of blood in our city. Follow me."

Angel became the leader of blood donation in his city. The members of his congregation currently donate blood six times a year. Angel invited other churches and pastors to take part in the blood drive. Now several churches compete to be the church that gives the most blood each year. As a result, La Paz now leads the state in blood acquisitions, and the new director of the blood bank received a government award for the spike in donations. Angel made that state official look like a genius. As a result, that man wants Angel to be successful.

Angel was pleased with this success, but wanted to take it to another level. He and Esther began to do outreaches to some of the Indian villages on the mainland of Mexico. They began to teach their people to serve the poor and love those who could do nothing to return the favor. Now, their church is not like an American church; material resources are scarce, and people live modest lives. Angel taught his people to give and serve in ways that seemed impossible to the natural mind. They are now taking their own people to new heights of love, service, and sacrifice. They are exporting miracles, healing, and generosity to the states around them.

Staying true to form, Angel got another "God idea" to make an impact on his city. His children go to a Catholic private school in La Paz. The school has an orphanage associated with it, and the priest from the school is involved with the orphanage as well. Angel learned that one of their greatest needs was for new shoes. Now, Mexican Protestants and Catholics are like cats and dogs. They do not get along. They do not fellowship together and cannot seem to find much value in each other. But when Angel returned to his congregation and shared that the Catholic orphanage needed shoes, his church decided to buy enough pairs of new shoes for all the orphans—70 pairs. They didn't buy cheap shoes, either; they bought Nikes. A local shoe store owner, who was not a believer, found out about their gesture and said he wanted in on the deal. He agreed to sell the shoes to the church at cost.

Angel's church was so excited about blessing the Catholic orphans that they invited the children to come to their church on a Sunday morning so they could present the gifts as a family. The priest and the children didn't know what Angel's church was up to, but unexpectedly the priest agreed to bring all his children to the Seeds of Life Protestant church on a Sunday morning. Such a thing had probably never happened in Mexican history!

The church wanted the Catholic children to feel the honor and love God has for them. Families that Angel and Esther knew could not afford to buy bikes for their own children pooled their money and gave a bike to the orphanage. They lined chairs across the front of the church and had the children sit in the chairs, facing the congregation. The people came and washed the feet of the children and then presented them with their new shoes. Then the children from Angel's church stood behind their guests and prophesied over them. Tears flowed from everyone in the room. Angel then invited the priest to sit in a chair. He washed the feet of the priest in front of his people. The priest could not believe what he and his children were experiencing. No one would ever be the same.

The school of ministry in La Paz continues to grow and the church continues to build new structures to expand their capacity. They are building teams for healing, the prophetic, and the working of miracles, and are also teaching their people about Heaven and the supernatural. This is all quickly becoming the normal Christian life for them. Outreach to the city is flowing, and miracles are happening in local environments. Heaven is invading everyday life in La Paz.

Angel and Esther continue to grow in their own faith and character. They are learning about love and intimacy for each other and their family. They are learning about cultivating freedom and honor as leaders. They are leading in creating a safe place for people who learned that life is about survival. They are challenging an impoverished culture to pull on the unlimited resources of Heaven. They are connecting the powerless with power, the hopeless with hope, and the captives with freedom. The transformation they are living is now becoming a transforming reality to those around them. They are catalysts for Heaven.

REFLECT

As you read the story of Angel and Esther, what stands out the most? What aspect of their testimony most challenges the way you have typically thought about ministry or outreach? Why?

_____

_____

_____

_____

Have you ever done something purely to make another person look good, as Angel did with the blood donations official? How did this make the other person feel? What was the overall result?

_____

_____

_____

_____

BUILDING A VESSEL OF HONOR

Those of us who have experienced the current revival know about the miracles that are happening. We see them increasing every day all around the world. Now we must build a vessel to transform our communities, our cities, and our nations. Global revival will not have lasting impact unless we see the core values of Heaven show up in our nation's governments. I don't mean that we simply elect people who say they are believers and go to church. I mean that we build a paradigm that invites a nation to be saved in a day, and we put into government those who will protect what is important to us.

Currently, we elect national leaders who will protect our economy, our safety, and our rights. The key ingredient that is missing is a government that will protect the priorities of Heaven and the presence of God in our land. Sometimes we like to believe that we are doing that in our churches; but there is one glaring reality: God's presence and power are missing from many of them. We are simply creating church governments that protect our precious traditions and theologies. The supernatural is nowhere near most of the largest denominations in our land. How stupid would unbelievers have to be to partner with the Church in making the entire country as limited as most churches are?

The culture of honor is not about giving the Church's leaders more control. I hope I have made it clear that it is actually about getting rid of control and cultivating self-control and freedom. The Church is to lead in bringing more freedom to the earth. Heaven is begging to invade the prison so many people live in, whether it is depression, pain, disease, or fear. Our role is to eliminate those things in our lives, homes, and church communities so we can lead others to the peace, joy, freedom, and love we've found for ourselves.

Honor is a powerful factor in holding on to what Heaven is pouring into our generation. Without an increase in the practice of loving, honoring relationships that emphasize unlimited freedom and opportunity for all involved, we will most likely watch this revival pass through our hands and have to be reinitiated by another generation. We have been privileged to live in such a beautiful moment in the history of humankind. Let's honor it!

REFLECT

What might it look like to elect government leaders who protect Heaven's priorities?

_____

_____

_____

_____

TOOL: TRANSFORMING YOUR CITY

1. From the wealth mindset, determine to proactively nourish and strengthen the society around you.

   - Outside of those who directly benefit you (your family, co-workers, and church community), identify people who can be a target of your honor.

   - Look for unbelievers whom you can regularly honor with your words and actions, even though their beliefs and lifestyles may be very different from yours (and are probably even sinful). Consider a practical strategy for how to love and honor those who are living in sin, and begin walking it out.

   - Identify the person in your life who disagrees with you the most intensely. Consider ways to cultivate a relationship of honor with that person. What can you do to express love and honor without trying to force agreement?

2. Make a plan for your strategic involvement in the transformation of your city.

    ▪ Ask God to give you creative and practical ways in which you can do things that will help bring transformation (like the example of Angel and Esther in La Paz).

    ▪ Connect with others who are also passionate about city transformation. Form alliances with others who are committed to impacting your city with honor. Meet often with these people to strengthen and encourage each other, as well as brainstorm new ideas for city impact.

    ▪ Identify the most influential leader in your city who is also open to a relationship of honor with you. Make a practical plan for how you can serve this person well, with love and honor.

DISCUSS

Discuss these questions with a friend or in a small group:

1. Do you resonate with the question, "How in the world are we ever going to do this in our church?" What obstacles do you see? What have you learned from this book that will help? What practical steps can you take to introduce this new culture in your home, work, and church environments?

2. Discuss the movement from revolution to reformation to transformation. Have you seen these in your life? In what ways? What sacred cows need to be barbecued in your life and church in order for this to happen?

3. What is it about the priorities of the pastoral government that make it an inferior Christianity? What about this concept, if anything, are you struggling to accept or understand?

APPLY

1. Do something outside of your comfort zone—something that costs you something—to purposefully partner with the priorities of Heaven and the culture of honor. It could be going on a "treasure hunt," visiting a church that models the

culture of honor, acting on a creative idea for how you can serve a public official to make him or her look like a genius, etc.

2. Prayerfully make a list of the sacred cows in your life. Ask God to renew your mind about these things according to Heaven's priorities (in ways, of course, that don't contradict the Bible). Next to your first list, write down what God says. Post this list somewhere that you will see it often as a daily reminder of your new set of priorities.

3. Write down which areas of honor are lacking or weak in your life. What can you do to begin strengthening these values and renewing your mind to Heaven's priorities? Write out some actions steps and share them with your spouse or a close friend. Ask God for divine strategy and the grace to step into the new things that He wants to do in and through your life.

ENDNOTES

1. Ann Hagedorn, *Beyond the River: The Untold Story of the Heroes of the Underground Railroad* (New York: Simon and Schuster, 2002), 274.

2. Ibid., 22.

3. Ibid., 23.

4. Ibid., 99.

ALSO BY DANNY SILK

Loving Our Kids On Purpose video and audio training sessions and workbook
www.LovingOnPurpose.com

Here is a fresh look at the age-old role of parenting. *Loving Our Kids on Purpose* brings the principles of the Kingdom of God and revival into our strategy as parents. This six-hour training set is available in both DVD and CD. It also has a companion workbook for classroom and small group training.

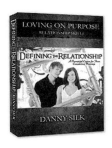

Defining the Relationship: A Premarital Course for Those Considering Marriage
www.LovingOnPurpose.com

Within this 9 session series you will find Danny's comedic style of presenting, as well as a serious attempt to bring couples into a reality check about their decision toward marriage. The *goal* of this series is to impart *courage*—courage to push through the challenging realities of the relationship or courage to walk away from the relationship. Also excellent for singles and married couples as well.

Cultura de Honor by Danny Silk - Spanish version of Culture of Honor

Amando A Nuestros Hijos A Proposito by Danny Silk - Spanish version of Loving Our Kids on Purpose

Children's Books:

The Chicken Coop Kid: A Silk Family Story by Danny and Sheri Silk

Shorts in the Snow: A Silk Family Story by Danny and Sheri Silk

One of Those Days A Silk Family Story by Danny and Sheri Silk

RECOMMENDED READING

A Life of Miracles by Bill Johnson

Basic Training for the Prophetic Ministry by Kris Vallotton

Basic Training for the Supernatural Ways of Royalty by Kris Vallotton

Developing a Supernatural Lifestyle by Kris Vallotton

Dreaming With God by Bill Johnson

Face to Face With God by Bill Johnson

Here Comes Heaven by Bill Johnson and Mike Seth

Loving Our Kids on Purpose by Danny Silk

Purity: The New Moral Revolution by Kris Vallotton

Release the Power of Jesus by Bill Johnson

Strengthen Yourself in the Lord by Bill Johnson

The Happy Intercessor by Beni Johnson

The Supernatural Power of a Transformed Mind by Bill Johnson

The Supernatural Ways of Royalty by Kris Vallotton and Bill Johnson

The Ultimate Treasure Hunt by Kevin Dedmon

When Heaven Invades Earth by Bill Johnson

IN THE RIGHT HANDS, THIS BOOK WILL CHANGE LIVES!

Most of the people who need this message will not be looking for this book. To change their lives, you need to put a copy of this book in their hands.

> *But others (seeds) fell into good ground, and brought forth fruit, some a hundred-fold, some sixty-fold, some thirty-fold* (Matthew 13:8).

Our ministry is constantly seeking methods to find the good ground, the people who need this anointed message to change their lives. Will you help us reach these people?

> *Remember this—a farmer who plants only a few seeds will get a small crop. But the one who plants generously will get a generous crop* (2 Corinthians 9:6).

EXTEND THIS MINISTRY BY SOWING
3 BOOKS, 5 BOOKS, 10 BOOKS, OR MORE TODAY,
AND BECOME A LIFE CHANGER!

Thank you,

Don Nori Sr., Founder
Destiny Image
Since 1982

DESTINY IMAGE PUBLISHERS, INC.

"Promoting Inspired Lives."

VISIT OUR NEW SITE HOME AT
WWW.DESTINYIMAGE.COM

FREE SUBSCRIPTION TO DI NEWSLETTER

Receive free unpublished articles by top DI authors, exclusive

discounts, and free downloads from our best and newest books.

Visit www.destinyimage.com to subscribe.

Write to: Destiny Image
                P.O. Box 310
                Shippensburg, PA 17257-0310

Call: 1-800-722-6774

Email: orders@destinyimage.com

For a complete list of our titles or to place an order
online, visit www.destinyimage.com.

FIND US ON FACEBOOK OR FOLLOW US ON TWITTER.

www.facebook.com/destinyimage   facebook
www.twitter.com/destinyimage   twitter